100 Poets: Passions of the Imperial Court

Hyakunin Isshu

Kazuya Takaoka

Mutsuo Takahashi

Yukikazu Ito

Emiko Miyashita

Michael Dylan Welch

Hyakunin Isshu
Book and cover design © 2008 Kazuya Takaoka
Selection and text copyright © 2008 Mutsuo Takahashi
Photographs copyright © 2008 Ito Yukikazu
English text copyright © 2008 Emiko Miyashita and Michael Dylan Welch
Published by PIE BOOKS

All rights reserved. No part of this publication may be reproduced in any form or by any means, graphic, electronic or mechanical, including photocopying and recording by an information storage and retrieval system, without permission in writing from the publisher.

PIE BOOKS
2-32-4, Minami-Otsuka, Toshima-ku, Tokyo 170-0005 Japan
Tel: +81-3-5395-4811 Fax: +81-3-5395-4812
http://www.piebooks.com
e-mail: editor@piebooks.com e-mail: sales@piebooks.com

ISBN978-4-89444-757-8 C0072
Printed in Japan

百人一首

アートディレクション
高岡一弥

文・解説
高橋睦郎

写真
伊藤之一

英訳
宮下惠美子
マイケル・ディラン・ウェルチ

『百人一首』いまむかし

高橋睦郎

　日本の古典の精髄を手っ取り早く読むことのできる一冊は何かと問われたら、一頃前までなら多くの識者が『百人一首』と答えたのではないだろうか。

　そればかりではない。多少とも子供の教育に関心のある家庭なら、まだもの心ついたかつかぬ小児との寝物語に、添寝の大人が一晩に一首を憶えさせて、情操の涵養に努めることが、ごくふつうにおこなわれた。また、お正月の家族や客人を交えての代表的な遊びは『百人一首』の歌留多取りだった。これは『百人一首』の一首一首の歌の上の句を記した読み札を読み手が読み、その上の句につづく下の句を作者の絵姿とともに記した取り札を、畳の上に散らばった中から取り手たちが競って取るという遊びである。『百人一首』こそがこの国の庶民の最低限の教養だったのだ。

　『百人一首』、正確な名は『小倉百人一首』。鎌倉時代初期の代表歌人藤原定家が七十四歳の時、隠棲先の洛西嵯峨の小倉山荘で、嫡男為家の舅蓮生入道宇都宮頼綱の依頼で、蓮生の山荘の障子を飾る色紙型のため、王朝時代を代表する歌人百人の代表歌一首ずつを選んで染筆したもの。百人は大和朝時代の天智・持統の父女二代の天皇に始まって当代の後鳥羽・順徳父子の天皇まで、五百数十年のあいだのさまざまの運命を生きた歌人たちだ。

　日本の王朝時代とは、形の上で天皇が頂点に立って国を治めた時代をいう。もともと大和地方の諸豪族の力の均衡の上に推戴されて不安定だった天皇が、とにもかくにも安定した力を得たきっかけはのちに天智天皇となる中大兄皇子が、新興の中臣氏の協力を得て旧勢力のうち最も強力な蘇我氏本流を滅ぼしたことだ。持

統天皇はその女(むすめ)で、天智天皇の皇太弟大海人皇子のちの天武天皇に嫁ぎ、王朝を堅めた女帝。そして、後鳥羽天皇のち上皇は、皇室を脅かす存在となった鎌倉幕府を討とうとして敗れ、息子の順徳天皇のち上皇とともに王朝時代を終焉に到らしめた帝王だ。

　王朝時代を動かした倫理は何だったかというと、それは恋の倫理だった。それは王朝の頂点に立つ天皇が祭司王だったことに由来する。何の祭司かといえば、稲と人に代表される生命力の持続増大のための祭司だ。稲をはじめとする植物の、人をはじめとする動物の生命力の持続増大のためには、動植物の生命力の発動を促し励ますべく、自ら恋に励まなければならない。天皇の側近く仕える公家たちも、天皇の恋を煽るべく恋に精出さなければならない。

　ところで、当時の恋は基本的に妻問い(＝妻訪い)というかたちを取る。これは処女はみだりに他家の男と言葉を交わさず、言葉を交わすことはすなわち情を通じることを意味するという、当時の共通認識(コンセンサス)によっている。上層階級の場合は妻問いは歌によってなされる。ある家に美しい娘がいるという噂が立つ。噂を聞いた若い男は求愛の歌を贈る。贈られた側で対応に当たるのは娘に付いている、男女関係の経験を積んだ侍女だ。彼女は男の歌にただちに答えたりはしない。

　焦がれた男は求愛の歌を贈りつづける。娘の側では男を値踏みして付き合ってもよいかと判断すると、求愛を受けるとも受けないとも取れる歌を返す。何度目かのやりとりののち、はじめて娘

自身が歌を返す。男は娘の部屋の外まで来ることを許され、ここでも歌を交わす。こういうことがつづいた後、愛の出会いが闇の中でおこなわれる。愛が交わされたのち、男は夜の明ける前に出なければならない。これを後朝(きぬぎぬ)という。後朝の後、男は歌を贈り、女は答えたり答えなかったり。やがて女の家族による所現(ところあら)わしということがあって、二人はやっと男女関係を認められる。

　天皇が後宮に妃嬪を多数抱えるのも、殿上人たちが後宮の女房たちに戯れかかるのも、以上のヴァリエーションといっていいだろう。現在の目から見れば乱倫とも見えるが、乱倫寸前で押しとどめていたものは、天皇を含めて男性の女性に対する尊敬の態度だろう。たとえば殿上人の後宮女房に対する対応の場合、女房たちは殿上人たちよりも何階級も下の受領(ずりょう)階級であるにもかかわらず、彼らは彼女らに対して敬語と丁寧語で対している。このことにより、彼女たちのありようは誇り高く、ひいては彼らのそれも誇り高くなる。これが雅び(＝宮び)、宮廷風の本質にほかならない。

　この雅びという名の宮廷文化は、綺羅星のごとき人物を産み、作品を産んだ。紫式部と『源氏物語』を、清少納言と『枕草子』を、道綱母と『蜻蛉日記』を、和泉式部と『和泉式部日記』を、在原業平と『伊勢物語』を、紀貫之と『土佐日記』を、菅原道真と『菅家文草』を、藤原公任と『和漢朗詠集』を、大江匡房と『江家次第』を、大僧正慈円と『愚管抄』を等等。

　そして、もちろん歌の国家的詩華集の『万葉集』を、『古今集』『後撰集』『拾遺集』『後拾遺集』『金葉集』『詞花集』『千載集』

『新古今集』から成る八大集を。『万葉集』は天武天皇の遺志を体現した持統女帝が下命し編集させた小アンソロジーをもとに、すべてで四度の編集拡充を経て出来上がったものだが、政治的には勅撰集となりそこねた。いわば前勅撰集。そこで勅撰集はほぼ百年後の延喜五年（九〇五）撰上された『古今集』に始まる。

　勅撰集は『古今集』を第一として第二十一の『新続古今集』まで、五百数十年のあいだ出つづける。しかし、実質的に勅撰集といえるのは第八の『新古今集』までで、幕府の意向を無視しては成立しえなくなった第九の『新勅撰集』からは正確には勅撰集とは言い難い。以後第二十一までの十一冊を十一代集と呼んで八大集と区別するのは、理由のあることなのだ。十一代集の始まりの『新勅撰集』の「新勅撰」とは、この集から勅撰の意味が新しくなり、大きく変わったということの表白かもしれない。

　『新勅撰集』は藤原定家の単独撰だ。しかし、その成立事情は複雑で、親幕派の関白藤原道家（みちいえ）から打診を受けた当初、定家は鎌倉幕府に破れて流刑中の後鳥羽院・順徳院の処遇がむつかしいことを理由に辞退している。最終的には受け入れ定家単独で撰んだものの、関白道家は摂政教実（のりざね）と合議の上、後鳥羽院以下宮方百首を落とし、幕府関係の七十首を加えている。その時点ではまだ両院の還京の可能性があったのだが、幕府側の拒否に遇い両院の名誉回復の望みは絶たれた。

　そこで、天智・持統両帝に始まり、後鳥羽・順徳両上皇で終わる『小倉百人一首』の構想は最終的に固まった、と推測される。

ついでにいえば、天智・持統両帝につづくのは柿本人麻呂と山部赤人の両宮廷歌人、そして後鳥羽・順徳両上皇の前は定家と藤原家隆の両宮廷詩人。そこから見える定家の意図は、天智・持統両帝に始まった王朝時代は、後鳥羽・順徳両院で終わった、この王朝時代は和歌の黄金時代で、それを側面から支えたのが代代の宮廷歌人で、最初が人麻呂・赤人なら最後は定家・家隆、そのあいだには帝王あり、殿上人あり、下級公家あり、武家あり、高僧あり、法師あり、貴夫人あり、女房あり、また遊芸の徒あり、彼らすべての一人一首、百人百首をもって一大葬送曲を編み、王朝時代、和歌の黄金時代を葬送しよう、ということだろう。

　こうして出来上がった『小倉百人一首』はわずか百首から成る軽少な一冊ながら、王朝時代の和歌を極限まで精撰したものとして、あの大部な『源氏物語』と拮抗する、日本古典の二つの代表の一つになった、と言っていいのではないか。これは定家の子孫が二条・京極・冷泉三家に分かれて、中世から近世にわたって歌壇を支配したことに大きな理由があろうが、二条家つづいて京極家が断絶、冷泉家の影響がほとんどなくなった近代以降も人気はいっこう衰えず、出されつづけ読まれつづけている。『小倉百人一首』が現在に生きる卓れた古典である、何よりの証拠だろう。

　『百人一首』は王朝時代の恋する宮廷が生んだ恋の歌のアンソロジーである。ところが、その中には一見したところ、恋の歌というより季節の歌といったほうがよさそうな歌も含まれる。これはどう考えればよいのだろうか。その答はこの国の歌の主宰者で

ある天皇が、稲と人に代表される生命力の持続増大のための祭司王だったという出発点に含まれている。生命力全般の祭司王である天皇の恋は、人に向かうとともに自然全体に向かう。これに準（なら）って、殿上人以下歌びとたちの恋も、人に向かうとともに、花に、鳥に、月に、雪に、あらゆる生命の動き、季節の変相に向かう。これが『百人一首』が季の歌を多く含む理由である。

　では、王朝時代の終わりから八百年近くを経た二十一世紀の日本の歌と天皇の関係はどうなのか。形の上ではいまなおこの国の歌の一年は天皇の主宰するところとなっている。年頭に宮中でおこなわれる御歌会始の儀が、それだ。そこではあらかじめ出された御題のもと、天皇の御製を筆頭に、皇后、皇太子、皇族方、召人、選者たち、そして国民一般の歌が朗詠される。

　そこで朗詠される歌は御製をはじめとして、恋の歌というよりも季の歌であることがほとんど、季の歌のヴァリエーションとしての時事詠も少なくない。しかし、季の歌が恋の歌の一種であることを思えば、御歌会始は『百人一首』が凍結した王朝時代という名の歌の黄金時代の遠い裔ということができよう。

　そのことに肯定的か否定的かに関わりなく、『百人一首』にこの国のありようの鍵が匿されていることは否みようがないのではないか。

書・本阿彌光悦

Hyakunin Isshu: The Past and the Present   Mutsuo Takahashi

When asked to name one book by which to quickly and easily appreciate the heart of Japanese classical literature, I believe many intellectuals would have recommended the *Hyakunin Isshu*, at least until recently. Not only that, but among families interested in educating their children, it had long been common to have them memorize its poems while they were still very young. When putting a little child to sleep each night, a parent would repeat the poems to help the child remember them by heart, and thereby cultivate an appreciation for poetry, history, and aesthetics. Furthermore, the most popular game played with guests at the New Year holiday had been *Hyakunin Isshu karuta*. To play the game, a reciter read out the first half of a poem on a *karuta* card, and participants were to complete the poem, choosing from cards spread over *tatami* mats by finding the matching *karuta* card with a picture of the poet and the second half of the poem. Thus, it can be said that the *Hyakunin Isshu* was a minimum cultural staple among the Japanese people.

The proper name of the so-called *Hyakunin Isshu* is *Ogura Hyakunin Isshu*. The collection was compiled by the leading *waka* poet in the early Kamakura Period, Fujiwara no Teika (1162-1241), when he was seventy-four years old. At the time, after his retirement, he lived in Ogurasanso, which was the name of his mountain villa located in Saga, west of Kyoto. Rensho Nyudo Utsunomiya Yoritsuna, who was the father-in-law of Teika's son, Tameie, asked Teika to select one hundred poets to represent Japan's dynastic age and to inscribe each of their poems on a *shikishigata*, a square paper, to decorate the screen doors of Yoritsuna's mountain villa.

Poems appeared in pairs throughout the collection, starting with the Yamato Dynasty's Emperor Tenji and Empress Jito, who were father and daughter, from the seventh century. The collection ended with a pair of poems by Emperor Go-Toba and Emperor Juntoku, father and son, who reigned during Teika's day at the turn of the thirteenth century. The *Ogura Hyakunin Isshu* therefore spans more than five hundred years in the dynastic era and celebrates the lives of poets who lived their various fortunes.

The dynastic age in Japan was the period when an Emperor formally reigned over the country, balancing the powers of various lords. At one point, Prince Nakanooe, who became

Emperor Tenji, was able to destroy the main stream of the most powerful old clan, the Soga family. His daughter married his brother, Prince Ōama, who later became Emperor Tenmu, and she stabilized the cherished dynastic age by becoming Empress Jitō. Emperor Go-Toba, later Retired Emperor Go-Toba, tried to subjugate the Kamakura Shogunate, which was beginning to threaten the Imperial Household, but failed. As a result, the dynastic age ended with Go-Toba and his son, Emperor Juntoku, later the Retired Emperor Juntoku.

One may ask, what ethics, morals, or code of conduct moved the dynastic age? It was the ethics of love. This motivation derives from the fact that Emperors during the dynastic age were also the chief performers of religious ceremonies. Their main religious role was to carry out ceremonies to increase the vital force represented by plants and animals. To strengthen the vital force of plants, symbolized by rice plants, and to proliferate animals, symbolized by humans, the Emperor was deeply occupied with lovemaking to encourage plant and animal procreation. Court nobles who served close to the Emperor were to work hard on their own lovemaking to reinforce the Emperor's love.

Marriage at that time took the form of *tsumadoi*, or visiting one's wife at night (a duolocal marriage). The consensus of the period was that a maiden did not exchange words with a man outside her family, because to do so was considered equivalent to having intercourse with him, therefore *tsumadoi* was arranged by the exchange of *waka* poems among the upper class.

When a rumour circulated that a beautiful maiden lived in a certain household, an interested man who heard the rumour would send her his courting *waka* poems. At the maiden's side, a lady in waiting who was experienced in love affairs would respond. She would not react immediately but would take her time. The man yearning for the maiden would keep sending his love poems. The lady in waiting would evaluate the suitor and, once he was approved as a candidate, the lady in waiting would return a poem that could be interpreted in two ways, both as acceptance and rejection. After such poems were exchanged several times, the maiden would send the man her own poem for the first time. The man would then be allowed to come to the outside of the maiden's room, and there they would exchange more poems. After several such occasions, they would then exchange love in the darkness. After making love to the maiden, the man had to leave before the day broke. This was called *kinuginu*, the morning after. After *kinuginu*, the man would send another poem to his love, and she might or might not answer back. If she responded favourably, the maiden's family would later hold a wedding ceremony called *tokoroarawashi*, and finally the man and the maiden would be admitted as a couple.

Variations of this scenario included the Emperor having a number of lovers in addition to the Empress Consort in the inner palace, and Court gentlemen flirting with Court ladies who attended there. From our standard of morals, their conducts may seem immoral. However, they stayed within moral limits of the time, indicated by the attitude of respect shown by the Emperor and Court gentlemen towards Court ladies. For example, in spite of the fact that Court ladies ranked below the Court gentlemen, the Court gentlemen used honorific and polite language towards Court ladies. Thus, the Court ladies were able to keep their pride, which sometimes exceeded the pride of the Court gentlemen. This is the very essence of *miyabi*, or to be Court-like or elegant, following the way of courtiers.

This Court culture, *miyabi*, nurtured a range of writers and poets who produced works that stood out like elegant silk garments or bright stars. Murasaki Shikibu wrote *Genji no Monogatari* ("The Tail of Genji"), Sei Shōnagon wrote *Makura no Sōshi* ("The Pillow Book"), Michitsuna no Haha wrote *Kagerō no Nikki* ("The Gossamer Diary"), Izumi Shikibu wrote *Izumi Shikibu no Nikki* ("Izumi Shikibu Diary"), Ariwara no Narihira became the model of *Ise no Monogatari* ("The Tales of Ise"), Ki no Tsurayuki wrote *Tosa no Nikki* ("Tosa Diary"), Sugawara Michizane wrote *Kanke Bunsō* (a collection of his poems and prose written in Chinese), Fujiwara no Kintō wrote *Wakan Rōei Shū* ("Japanese and Chinese Poems to Sing"), Ōe no Masafusa wrote *Gōkeshidai* (a detailed record of government affairs and ceremonies in the Imperial Court), and Daisōjō Jien wrote *Gukanshō* ("A Selection of the Opinions of a Fool"), among many other works.

And of course, we should not forget the *Man'yōshū* ("Collection of Ten Thousand Leaves"), which is the oldest national anthology of written poetic expression. Nor should we forget the first eight *waka* anthologies compiled by Imperial command: *Kokinshū*, *Gosenshū*, *Shūishū*, *Goshūishū*, *Kin'yōshū*, *Shiikashū*, *Senzaishū*, and *Shin Kokinshū*.

Originally, the *Man'yōshū* was a small anthology edited at the command of Empress Jitō to follow the will of the late Emperor Tenmu. The anthology went through four editions of revision and amplification before its completion, but it failed politically to be qualified as a *chokusenshū*, an official anthology of poems collected by Imperial command. In a way, it may be called a *pre-chokusenshū*. The era of *chokusenshū* began about a hundred years later, with the first anthology complied by Imperial command, *Kokinshū*, in the fifth year of the Engi Era (905).

Twenty-one *chokusenshū* were compiled over a period of more than five hundred years, counting *Kokinshū* as the first, and the *Shin Shoku Kokinshū* as the twenty-first. To be precise, however, only the first eight anthologies, until the *Shin Kokinshū*, can be claimed as proper *chokusenshū*. Starting with the ninth anthology, Shin Chokusenshū, the interference by the Kamakura Shogunate became obvious and thus it is hard to say that they truly qualified as being compiled by Imperial command. The last eleven anthologies including the twenty-first are grouped together and referred to as "The Eleven Anthologies" because they are considered different from the first eight *chokusenshū*. An indication of this change is that the title given to the ninth anthology is *Shin (new) Chokusen*, meaning that the *chokusen* had been drastically revised.

The *Shin Chokusenshū* was complied by Fujiwara no Teika. However, the process of its completion was rather complicated. When the Chancellor, Fujiwara no Michiie, who supported the Kamakura Shogunate, asked Teika to compile this collection, Teika declined the offer. This was because he thought it was very delicate to handle the matter of Retired Emperor Go-Toba and Retried Emperor Juntoku, who had fought and lost against the Kamakura Shogunate and were condemned to exile. But he eventually accepted the offer and compiled the anthology by himself. However, Chancellor Michiie and Regent Norizane consulted together and dropped a hundred *waka* poems written by Retired Emperor Go-Toba and his group of courtiers and instead added seventy poems written by Shogunate-related poets. Until that point, hope still remained for the return of both retired Emperors to the capital, but then the Shogunate government rejected the possibility. As a result, the hope for their restoration of honour was lost forever.

Hereupon we can assume that the idea of the *Ogura Hyakunin Isshu*, which begins with Emperor Tenji and Empress Jito, and ends with Retired Emperor Go-Toba and Retired Emperor Juntoku, was finally taking shape in Teika's mind.

It is of interest to note that the Court poets Kakinomoto no Hitomaro and Yamabe no Akahito follow the Emperor Tenji and Empress Jito, whereas Teika and Fujiwara no Ietaka, who were also the Court poets, appear before Go-Toba and Juntoku. One may wonder about Teika's intention by this symmetrical placement. Teika is saying that a period of the monarchic government or dynastic age began with the Emperor Tenji and Empress Jito and had come to an end with Retired Emperor Go-Toba and Retired Emperor Juntoku. This period was the golden age of *waka* poetry, sustained by generations of Court *waka* poets, beginning with Hitomaro and Akahito, and ending with Teika and Ietaka. In between were Emperors, courtiers, low-class aristocrats, warriors, high-class priests and monks, ladies, Court ladies, and entertainers. Employing one *waka* poem composed by each contributor, a hundred *waka* by a hundred poets, he composed a great funeral march to mourn the period of the monarchic government and the golden age of *waka* poetry.

Although the book is small and contains only a hundred *waka* poems, the *Ogura Hyakunin Isshu* holds the utmost selection of *waka* from the period of Japanese Court rule, which makes it equivalent in stature to the voluminous *Tale of Genji*. Indeed, together with *The Tale of Genji*, we might say that the *Ogura Hyakunin Isshu* is one of the two most significant contributions to classical Japanese literature.

We might assume that the long-lasting popularity of *Hyakunin Isshu* was due to Teika's descendants producing three *waka*-master families. The Nijyo, Kyogoku, and Reizei families had continued to rule *waka* circles during the mediaeval period and the early-modern period in Japan. However, the popularity of *waka* did not fade away after the extinction of the Nijō family followed by the Kyōgoku family, nor when the Reizei family lost its influence in the post early-modern period. The book has been widely and repeatedly published and read. The *Ogura Hyakunin Isshu* is undeniably a prominent classical collection that still thrives today.

The *Ogura Hyakunin Isshu* is an anthology of love, created out of the passions of Japanese Court life. Yet poems that seem more like seasonal poems than love poems are also included, and readers may wonder why. The answer can be found in the fact that the Emperor not only led the country's *waka* tradition, but also functioned as the country's highest officiating Shinto priest, enhancing and maintaining the vital force of life represented by rice plants and human beings. The passion of the officiating priest celebrates the overall vital force, and therefore focuses not only on humans but on all of nature. Following this model, the passion of the Court nobles and lower-ranking poets also focuses on cherry blossoms, birds, the moon, snow, all kinds of life phenomena, and the shift of seasons. This is why the *Ogura Hyakunin Isshu* contains so many poems on seasons.

After almost eight hundred years since the Court period ended, another question readers may ask is about the relationship between *waka* and the Emperor of twenty-first century Japan. Formally, traditional *waka* poetry is still led by the Emperor, as we see in the New Year's Poetry Reading Ceremony held at the Imperial Court at the beginning of each year. The Emperor's poem is chanted first, followed by poems of the Empress Consort, the Prince Imperial, the Imperial family of Japan, guest poets, the judges, and the public. The *waka* poems chanted at the ceremony, including the Emperor's *waka*, are today mostly about seasons rather than love. Other poems dwell on current events as a variation of the seasonal poem. If we think of these seasonal poems as a kind of love poem, professing a love of nature, we might see the New Year's Poetry Reading Ceremony as a distant echo of Japan's Court period and the golden age of *waka*, marvelously preserved and celebrated by the *Ogura Hyakunin Isshu*. Whether one agrees or disagrees with this perspective, I believe it to be undeniably true that a key to understanding the heart of Japan and its literature is sheltered in the *Ogura Hyakunin Isshu*.

Hyakunin Isshu

百人一首

a temporary lookout hut
by the ripening rice fields
has a rough rush-thatched roof—
my sleeves are kept
wet with the dews

aki no ta no kariho no io no toma wo arami
waga koromode wa tsuyu ni nuretsutsu　　*Tenji Tennō*

Emperor Tenji

秋の田のほとり、豊かに稔った稲を刈り干すための仮小屋は、苫の目も疎く葺かれているので、そこで夜番をする私の衣の袖は濡れどおしで、うつらうつらと仮眠もできない。

一

天智天皇(てんぢてんわう)

秋の田のかりほの庵の苫(とま)をあらみわが衣手(ころもで)は露にぬれつつ

spring is over
and summer must have come—
on heavenly Mount Kagu,
pure white clothes
are said to be drying

haru sugite natsu kinikerashi shirotae no
koromo hosuchō ama no kaguyama　　*Jitō Tennō*

Empress Jitō

どうやら春が過ぎて、夏が到来したようだ。新しい季節のしるしに白妙織(しろたえおり)の衣(ころも)を干すという聖なる香具山(かぐやま)に、白い色がまぶしい。この山に来た夏はたちまち全国に及ぶだろう。

二

持統天皇（ぢとうてんわう）

春すぎて夏来にけらし白妙（しろたへ）のころもほすてふ天（あま）のかぐ山

on a rugged mountain peak
a copper pheasant falls asleep
drooping its lengthy tail—
must I too sleep alone
through this long long night?

ashihiki no yamadori no o no shidario no
naganagashi yo wo hitori kamo nen　　Kakinomoto no Hitomaro

Kakinomoto no Hitomaro

山深く住む山鳥、その長く垂れた尾羽のように長長しく続くこの夜を、私はひとりさびしく寝るほかはないだろうか。恋しいあなたを遠くに置いて。

三

柿本人麻呂(かきのもとのひとまろ)

あしひきの山鳥(やまどり)の尾のしだり尾のながながし夜をひとりかも寝む

as I come out and look up
from the coast of Tagonoura,
the pure white snow keeps falling
on the lofty peak
of Mount Fuji

tagonoura ni uchiidete mireba shirotae no
fuji no takane ni yuki wa furitsutsu　　Yamabe no Akahito

Yamabe no Akahito

都から遠く旅を続け田子の浦に出てみると、雪の白妙の聖衣で覆われた富士の高い嶺に、さらに雪が降りつづいて。山の女神が嘉してくださっているのだ。

四

山部赤人(やまべのあかひと)

田子の浦にうち出(いで)てみれば白妙(しろたへ)の富士のたかねに雪はふりつつ

deep in the mountains
stepping through the fallen crimson leaves
a deer cries for his mate—
when I hear the voice
autumn melancholy deepens

okuyama ni momiji fumiwake naku shika no
koe kiku toki zo aki wa kanashiki   *Sarumaru Daifu*

Sarumaru, A Troupe Leader

奥山の萩は花も散り、いちめん黄葉。その萩黄葉を踏み分けるように、さらに山奥に入って行く雄鹿の妻恋いの声を聞く時、そうでなくともも悲しい秋が、いっそうもの悲しく感じられる。

五 猿丸大夫（さるまるだいふ）

おくやまにもみぢ踏み分け鳴く鹿の声聞くときぞ秋はかなしき

a heavenly bridge
of milky-feathered magpies—
the whiteness of frost
on the Imperial staircase
reminds me of night's deepening

kasasagi no wataseru hashi ni oku shimo no
shiroki wo mireba yo zo fukenikeru　　Chūnagon Yakamochi

Middle Counsellor Yakamochi

七夕の夜に牽牛を織女の許に渡すため、鵲が翼を連ねて天河に渡すという天上の橋。いまは冬、その鵲の橋さながら、後宮から主上の寝所につづく御階にまっ白に霜が降りて。夜は更ける限りまで更け、夜明けはもうそこまで来ている。

六　中納言家持

かささぎのわたせる橋に置く霜の白きを見れば夜ぞふけにける

when I raise my face
to look at the heavenly fields,
I see the same moon
that I saw arise in Kasuga
from Mount Mikasa

amanohara furisakemireba kasuga naru
mikasa no yama ni ideshi tsuki kamo　　*Abe no Nakamaro*

Abe no Nakamaro

いま私の前に広がる海原、その上にさらにひろびろと広がる天の原、その彼方、東の水平線にいましも月が出て来た。その月は水平線をさらにはるかに東にあるわが故国の都に、帝の上の天蓋のように鎮まる御蓋山の上にも出ている月。私にはありありと見えるのだ、その山影も、その上に出た月の姿も。

七
阿倍仲麿（あべのなかまろ）

あまの原ふりさけ見れば春日（かすが）なる御蓋（みかさ）の山にいでし月かも

my hut, if you ask,
is to the capital's southeast
where I live serenely—
yet people say I've renounced the world
only to live dismally in Mount Uji

waga io wa miyako no tatsumi shika zo sumu
yo wo ujiyama to hito wa iu nari　　*Kisen Hōshi*

Monk Kisen

この世は仮の世、その仮の世を過ごす私の仮住みの庵は都の東南の方角にある。これこのとおり、自分ではそれなりに心澄んだ日日のつもりだが、口さがない世の人びとは、世の中を憂しと思っての宇治山暮らしなどと噂しているらしい。やれやれおせっかいなことよ。

八

喜撰法師(きせんほふし)

わが庵は都のたつみしかぞ住む世をうぢ山と人はいふなり

the beauty of cherry blossoms
has passed its peak
in vain
while I looked idly
at the endless rain

hana no iro wa utsurinikeri na itazura ni
waga mi yo ni furu nagame seshi ma ni   Ono no Komachi

Ono no Komachi

目の前の花の色も、それを見ている私の色香も、すっかり移ろい褪せてしまったなあ。ただぼんやりとなすこともなく、降りつづく長雨を来る日も来る日もながめ、自分の身すぎ世すぎのことを思いつづけているあいだに。

九 小野小町(をののこまち)

花のいろはうつりにけりないたづらに我身(わがみ)世にふるながめせしまに

so this is the place
where all who come and go,
both friends and strangers,
meet again after parting—
the gate at Meeting Hill

kore ya kono yuku mo kaeru mo wakarete wa
shiru mo shiranu mo ōsaka no seki   Semimaru

Semimaru

さあ皆の衆、これが東へ行く人、都へ帰る人が行き別れ、知り人にも見知らぬ人にも会うという、人の行き来はげしい逢坂の関ですじゃ。心してお通りなさるがよいぞ。

一〇
蟬丸(せみまる)

これやこの行くも帰るも別れてはしるもしらぬもあふ坂の関

my boat has rowed out
on the vast expanse of waters
amid the eighty islands—
tell this to my loved one,
you who fish in fishing boats

watanohara yasoshima kakete kogiidenu to
hito ni wa tsuge yo ama no tsuribune　　Sangi Takamura

Consultant Takamura

水平線にむかって限りも知らず広がる大海
原。その上に点在する島から島へと、私の舟
が漕ぎ出して行ったと、なつかしい都びとら
に告げてくれよ、波に浮かぶ海人の釣舟よ。

一一 参議篁（さんぎたかむら）

わたのはら八十島（やそしま）かけてこぎいでぬと人には告げよ蜑（あま）のつりぶね

winds high in the sky
please blow and block
the gateway of clouds—
I wish to admire a little longer
the heavenly maidens' figures

amatsukaze kumo no kayoiji fukitoji yo
otome no sugata shibashi todomen   Sōjō Henjō

High Priest Henjō

吹く風よ、雲の通い路に関の戸を立てて閉じてくれよ。いま五節の舞を舞い終えた処女たちが、まるで天上にでも帰って行くかのように退下して行く。その華やかな姿をもうしばらくとどめておきたいのだ。

一二

僧正遍昭（そうじゃうへんぜう）

あまつ風くものかよひ路（ぢ）ふきとぢよ乙女のすがたしばしとどめむ

from the peak of Mount Tsukuba
the Man-Woman River started to flow—
so, too, my love has grown
from a thin stream
to a deepening pool

tsukubane no mine yori otsuru minanogawa
koi zo tsumorite fuchi to narinuru　　Yōzeiin

Retired Emperor Yōzei

いにしえ、男が歌いかけ女が答えられなかった時は、女が男の一夜妻にならなければならなかったという歌垣の山、筑波山。その男のみね・女のみねのあいだを激ち落ちる男女川の水を集めた淵のように、私のあなたへの激しい恋の思いも積もり積もって、怖ろしい淵となってしまった。覚悟なされよ。

一三
陽成院(やうぜいゐん)

筑波嶺(つくばみね)のみねより落つるみなの川こひぞつもりて淵(ふち)となりぬる

like Michinoku's Shinobu cloth
of randomly printed patterns,
my heart is in disarray—
who but you, dear,
is to blame?

michinoku no shinobumojizuri tare yue ni
midaresomenishi ware naranaku ni   Kawara no Sadaijin

The Kawara Minister of the Left

遠いみちのくの、音に名高い信夫の里のしのぶぐさで染めた捩り染めの摺衣。しのびにしのんだ私の心が捩り染めのように乱れはじめたのは、誰のせいでもなくあなたのせい。それなのにかえって私の心をお疑いとは。心外千万とはまさにこのことではありますまいか。

一四
河原左大臣(かはらのさだいじん)

みちのくのしのぶもぢずりたれゆゑに乱れそめにし我ならなくに

for you alone
I come out to the spring fields
to gather young herbs—
as I pick them, the snow keeps falling
onto my full sleeves

kimi ga tame harunono ni idete wakana tsumu
waga koromode ni yuki wa furitsutsu　　Kōkō Tennō

Emperor Kōkō

かつては神聖な処女が摘んで神に献げたという春の野に萌え出たばかりの神聖な若菜、それをゆかしいあなたにさし上げたく、私自ら春の野に出て摘んでいますと、衣の袖に雪が降りしきり、濡れてしまうほどなのです。

一五

光孝天皇(くわうかうてんわう)

君がため春の野にいでて若菜摘むわが衣手(ころもで)に雪は降りつつ

it is time to depart,
yet if I hear that you pine for me,
for the pines that grow
on the peak of Mount Inaba,
I shall return right away

tachiwakare inaba no yama no mine ni ouru
matsu to shi kikaba ima kaerikon   Chūnagon Yukihira

Middle Counsellor Yukihira

私はあなたに別れてこれから因幡の国に赴くが、その因幡山に生い繁る松にことよせ、待つと一言便りをよこしてくれるなら、何もかもうち捨ててそくざに帰って来たいと思っているよ。

一六
中納言行平
ちゅうなごんゆきひら

たちわかれいなばの山の峰におふるまつとしきかばいま帰りこむ

not known even in the reign of gods
mighty enough to penetrate a thousand rocks:
the beauty of Tatsuta River,
tie-dying the water
in foreign crimson

chihayaburu kamiyo mo kikazu tatsutagawa
karakurenai ni mizu kukuru to wa　　*Ariwara no Narihira no Ason*

Ariwara no Narihira, Court Noble

血が天から降って来るなどというようなことがあるだろうか。神神の時代にもそんなことは聞いたことがない。大和を貫流する蛇身のその名も龍田の川を血の唐紅のくくり染めにして流れていこうとは。大和の地霊が山城の地霊に敗れ、わが平成王朝は瓦解してしまった。その敗けいくさが秋ごとに川のおもてに繰り返されるのだ。

一七

在原業平朝臣（ありはらのなりひらのあそん）

ちはやふる神代もきかず龍田川（たつたがは）からくれなゐに水くくるとは

the waves washing
the shores of Suminoe—
even at night, in my dream,
on the passage that carries me to you
I hesitate, avoiding to be seen

suminoe no kishi ni yoru nami yoru sae ya
yume no kayoiji hitome yokuran　　Fujiwara no Toshiyuki no Ason

Fujiwara no Toshiyuki, Court Noble

かつて難波京があり殷賑を極めたという住の江の浦。そこにひた寄せてくる波のように、ひたすらにあなたに寄り添い一つになりたいと思っている私なのに、どうしたことか、夜の夢の中のあなたの許に通う路でさえ、つい人目を避けてしまうのだ。

一八　藤原敏行朝臣

住の江の岸による波よるさへやゆめのかよひ路人めよくらむ

are you saying you won't see me
in this lifetime,
not even as briefly
as between the joints in the reeds
at Naniwa lagoon?

naniwagata mijikaki ashi no fushinoma mo
awade kono yo wo sugushite yo toya　Ise

Ise

いったい何ごとがあって、これほどお逢いすることがむつかしいのでしょうか、あの琵琶湖を出た大河淀川の海にそそぐ難波潟、水面いちめんに生い繁る芦の節と節の間のように短い夏の夜も、あなたなしの独り臥しでこの夜を過ごせ、とおっしゃるのでしょうか。

一九　伊勢(いせ)

難波潟(なにはがた)みじかき芦のふしの間(ま)も逢はでこの世をすぐしてよとや

my depression has deepened
since our rumour circulated,
but to me it no longer matters—
like Naniwa's selfless channel markers,
I must sacrifice myself to see you

wabinureba ima hata onaji naniwa naru
mi wo tukushite mo awan to zo omou　Motoyoshi Shinnō

Prince Motoyoshi

あなたとの秘めごとが夜に露われてこのように思い悩んでいるからには、今はもうどうなっても同じこと。それならば難波潟に打ち込まれた澪標ではないが、この身が滅びつくすことになっても、恋の舟に身を乗せて標識の導く果てまであなたに逢いに行きたいものだ。

二〇
元良親王(もとよししんわう)

わびぬれば今はたおなじ難波(なには)なるみをつくしても逢はむとぞ思ふ

because you wrote
that you would come soon,
I have waited
till the rise of the morning moon
this ninth month

*imakonto iishi bakari ni nagatsuki no
ariakenotsuki wo machiidetsuru kana*　　Sosei Hōshi

Priest Sosei

いますぐ来ようとあなたがおっしゃったばかりに、その言葉を信じて来る夜も来る夜も待ちつづけるうち、肝腎(かんじん)のあなたはついに現れることなく、代わりにその名も長月の有明の月が出て、夜はしらじらと明けてしまったことです。

二一

素性法師(そせいほふし)

いま来(こ)むといひしばかりに長月(ながつき)の有明(ありあけ)の月を待ちいでつるかな

as it blows,
the autumn grass and trees
wither at once—
now I see why this mountain wind
is called a storm

fuku kara ni aki no kusaki no shiorureba
mube yamakaze wo arashi to iuran　　Fun'ya no Yasuhide

Fun'ya no Yasuhide

山にむかって見ていると、風が吹くとともに目に見えて秋の草木がしおれる。なるほど、山風とつづけて書けば嵐という字になるが、昔の人はつくづく巧く考えついたものだと感心してしまうねぇ。

二二
文屋(ふんやの)康秀(やすひで)

ふくからに秋の草木のしをるればむべ山風をあらしといふらむ

as I look at the moon,
my mind is torn to a thousand pieces,
sinking me into sadness,
although this autumn
is not for me alone

tsuki mireba chiji ni mono koso kanashikere
wagami hitotsu no aki ni wa aranedo　Ōe no Chisato

Ōe no Chisato

早霜（はやじも）が降り澄んだ空に深沈（しんちん）と冴えわたる月を眺めていると、幾千のもの、幾千のことが一つ一つ、ひしひしと悲しく身にしみる。凋落（ちょうらく）の秋は誰にも等しく訪れるものの、私ひとりに来るわけではないが、愛する人を亡くした私にはひとしおつらく思えるのです。

二三
大江千里(おほえのちさと)

月みればちぢに物こそかなしけれわが身ひとつの秋にはあらねど

on this pressing journey
I have no sacramental strips of silk
to offer the gods at Mount Tamuke
but its brocade of tinted leaves—
please accept them as you please

kono tabi wa nusa mo toriaezu tamukeyama
momiji no nishiki kami no manima ni   Kanke

The House of Sugawara

このたびの帝（みかど）にお伴（とも）しての旅立ちはいかにもあわただしく、旅の安全を祈るべきこの峠の道の神よ、あなたに献（たてまつ）るべき幣（ぬさ）の用意も叶（かな）いませんでした。しかし、さいわいここに見事な紅葉があります。この一枝の錦（にしき）をさし出しますが、ご嘉納（かのう）はみ心のままになさってください。

二四
菅家(くわんけ)

このたびはぬさもとりあへず手向山(たむけやま)もみぢのにしき神のまにまに

if you hold the power of your name,
oh Meeting Hill's sleep-together vine,
then I wish your charm
would haul my love in closer
unnoticed by anyone

na ni shi owaba ōsakayama no sanekazura
hito ni shirarede kuru yoshi mogana　　Sanjō no Udaijin

The Sanjō Minister of the Right

逢うて寝るという名を持つ逢坂山のさねかずらよ、お前の名が名のとおりなら、誰にも知られることなく蔓を手繰ってお前の許に辿り着き、逢うてそのまま共寝する、そんな手立てがあればよいのだが。ここに来るにも苦労の多いことだなあ。

二五
三条右大臣

名にし負はば逢坂山のさねかづら人に知られで来るよしもがな

Mount Ogura,
your peak covered with tinted leaves—
if you have a heart,
please stay tinted
till the next royal visit

ogurayama mine no momijiba kokoro araba
ima hitotabi no miyuki matanan   *Teishinkō*

Lord Teishin

小倉山よ、お前の装う見事な紅葉を今日、御幸あって上皇が賞でられ、み子の当今（醍醐天皇）にもお見せになりたい、とのありがたいお言葉を賜ったぞ。人ならぬお前にももし心というものがあるならば、この恩みに深く感じ、遠くない行幸まで散らすことなく、紅葉の美しさを保って、待っていてほしいものだ。

二六
貞信公(ていしんこう)

をぐらやま峰の紅葉(もみぢば)こころあらばいまひとたびのみゆきまたなむ

here on the Mika Plain
the River Izumi springs forth
and surges through—
when have I met you? I haven't,
yet I yearn for you as if I had

mikanohara wakite nagaruru izumigawa
itsumikitoteka koishikaruran　*Chūnagon Kanesuke*

Middle Counsellor Kanesuke

かつて何びとかが甕をいくつもいくつも埋めた、そのおびただしい甕の口が泉となって水が湧きあふれるという甕の原。その原をいくつにも分けて流れる水が一つになって奔流する泉川の、いったいいつ見たからお前がこんなに恋しいのだろうか、はじめて見た日の記憶さえさだかではないのに。

二七
中納言兼輔

みかの原わきてながるるいづみ川いつ見きとてか恋しかるらむ

in a mountain village
winter is the most lonely,
for the comings and goings
of all the people
dry up with the grasses

yamazato wa fuyu zo sabishisa masarikeru
hitome mo kusa mo karenu to omoeba　　*Minamoto no Muneyuki no Ason*

Minamoto no Muneyuki, Court Noble

私の住むこの山里はもともとさびしいところ。しかし、それでも、春は花見、夏は涼み、秋は紅葉狩と、それなりに愉しみもあり、人も集まるが、冬ともなるとまったく人目も離れ、誰にも見られることなく草も枯れてしまった。山里のさびしさここに極まれり、という風情だ。

二八

源宗于朝臣

山里は冬ぞさびしさまさりける人目も草もかれぬとおもへば

if I pluck
a white chrysanthemum,
I must pluck by guesswork
after the first frost
has disguised them

kokoroate ni oraba ya oran hatsushimo no
okimadowaseru shiragiku no hana　　Ōshikōchi no Mitsune

Ōshikōchi no Mitsune

白菊を折ろうかと思うのだが、何とか見当つけて折るほかはない。思いがけず早い初霜が降りて、霜の白と菊の白とが見分けがつかない今朝の前栽。それにしても、見事な霜、見事な菊。まるで霜が花で、菊が水の結晶であるかのようだ。

二九
凡河内躬恒（おほしかふちのみつね）

心あてに折らばや折らむはつ霜の置きまどはせるしらぎくの花

since our parting
when the morning moon
looked so indifferent,
no other time but dawn
makes me suffer

ariake no tsurenaku mieshi wakare yori
akatsuki bakari uki mono wa nashi　　Mibu no Tadamine

Mibu no Tadamine

夜が明けたのにまだ残っている有明月さながらに、私の思いはまだ残っているのに、あなたは前夜の睦言(むつごと)も忘れたかのようにつれなかったし、その後も逢ってくれようともしない。あの時以来、私にとって暁ほど憂鬱(ゆううつ)な時はなくなってしまった。こういつても、あなたには何の感情も動くまいが。

三〇

壬生忠岑(みぶのただみね)

有明(ありあけ)のつれなくみえしわかれより暁(あかつき)ばかり憂きものはなし

daybreak—
bright enough to suggest
it's the dawn moon,
the snow's whiteness
on Yoshino village

asaborake ariake no tsuki to miru made ni
yoshino no sato ni fureru shirayuki　Sakanoue no Korenori

Sakanoue no Korenori

ほのぼのと夜が明けそめ、有明月の光かと思ったら、なんと吉野の里いちめんに薄薄と降り敷いた初雪ではないか。初雪なのに旧（ふる）くから見知っているような気がしてならないのは、あの遠い世の聖帝天武天皇（てんむ）が吉野を拠点に挙兵された時に降って以来、めでたいことの予兆として尊ばれて来た吉野の雪だからだ。

三一

坂上是則（さかのうへのこれのり）

朝ぼらけ有明(ありあけ)の月と見るまでに吉野の里にふれるしら雪

the wind-placed weir
in a mountain stream
is, as it happens,
the tinted fallen leaves
unable to flow

yamagawa ni kaze no kaketaru shigarami wa
nagare mo aenu momiji narikeri　　*Harumichi no Tsuraki*

Harumichi no Tsuraki

ここ都の東北から比叡山と如意岳のあいだを通って、志賀寺へ出る志賀越えの山道から見ると、はるか下に見える谷川のはげしい流れをせき止めて、おびただしい紅葉がたまっている。ああ、あれは志賀越えの名に因み、人ならぬ風がかけた紅葉のしがらみなのだ。

三二

春道列樹(はるみちのつらき)

山川(やまがは)に風のかけたるしがらみは流れもあへぬもみぢなりけり

the light filling the air
is so mild this spring day
only the cherry blossoms
keep falling in haste—
why is that so?

hisakata no hikari nodokeki harunohi ni
shizugokoro naku hana no chiruran　　Ki no Tomonori

Ki no Tomonori

気の遠くなるほど久しい、天地開闢(かいびゃく)の時以来変わらぬ、広く深い空から降ってくる光の、身も心も溶けてしまいそうにのどかな、この春の日の真さかりに、いったい何のゆえなれば、こんなにも落ちつきなく、桜の花よ、お前は散りやまないのか。

三三
紀友則(きのとものり)

ひさかたのひかりのどけき春の日にしづ心なく花の散るらん

at my great age
when all my friends are gone,
with whom can I make friends?
even Takasago's ancient double pine tree
cannot be my friend

tare wo kamo shiruhito ni sen takasago no
matsu mo mukashi no tomo naranaku ni   Fujiwara no Okikaze

Fujiwara no Okikaze

かつて親しく交わり、時には感情の行き違いからいさかいもした友人たちもみんな死んで向う側に行き、私一人が老いて孤独に残っている。長生きで知られた峰の上に唯一本孤高に立っているという高砂の松なら友になってくれるかとはるばる訪ねてみたが、昔馴染みに代わる友となれたわけではない。

三四

藤原興風(ふぢはらのおきかぜ)

誰(たれ)をかもしる人にせん高砂(たかさご)の松もむかしの友ならなくに

I wonder about you
but cannot read your mind—
in this village where I used to visit,
the plum blossoms still smell sweetly
the way they always did

hito wa isa kokoro mo shirazu furusato wa
hana zo mukashi no ka ni nioikeru   Ki no Tsurayuki

Ki no Tsurayuki

人の心は変わりやすいと申しますから、あなたが私に対して心変わりなさったかどうかは、さあ存じません。それでも馴染みのこの里、この家は昔から変わらぬ梅のよい匂いで私を迎えてくれます。この匂いの誘いを拒める者がありましょうか。ええ、ええ、今晩はこちらに泊めていただきますとも。

三五
紀(きの)貫(つら)之(ゆき)

人はいさ心もしらずふるさとは花ぞむかしの香(か)ににほひける

the short summer night
begins to dawn, although it feels
like it is still evening—
where in the clouds
does the moon shelter

natsunoyo wa mada yoi nagara akenuru wo
kumo no izuko ni tsuki yadoruran　　Kiyohara no Fukayabu

Kiyohara no Fukayabu

短い夏の夜のこと。まだ宵の口だと思って月を眺めているうちに、夜が明けてしまい、ふと気づくと肝腎の月は見えなくなってしまっている。浮気者の月よ、私を置き去りにして、あかつき雲のいったいどこを仮の宿に雲がくれしてしまったのか。

三六
清原深養父(きよはらのふかやぶ)

夏の夜はまだ宵(よひ)ながら明けぬるを雲のいづこに月やどるらむ

in the autumn fields
the wind blows repeatedly
over the white dew—
each gust disperses
the pearls not strung

shiratsuyu ni kaze no fukishiku aki no no wa
tsuranukitomenu tama zo chirikeru   Fun'ya no Asayasu

Fun'ya no Asayasu

一晩じゅう吹き荒れた野分(のわき)の結果やいかにと、外に出てみた。これはまたどうだろう、いちめんに置いた白露にゆうべの名残の風がしきりに吹き、秋の野はらはまるで貫き糸に止めかねた水晶の玉が散り乱れているようで、秋の女神のなやましい肌(はだえ)を眼前にするかのようだ。

三七
文屋朝康
（ふんやのあさやす）

しらつゆに風の吹きしく秋の野はつらぬきとめぬ玉ぞ散りける

I should have known when we vowed
that I would be forgotten by you . . .
now that you have left me,
I worry about your life, you who swore
unchanging love before gods

wasuraruru mi woba omowazu chikaiteshi
hito no inochi no oshiku mo aru kana　　Ukon

Ukon

あれほど言葉を尽くして愛の誓いをしてくだすったあなたの訪れも、いつしか途絶えてしまった。それにつけても気にかかるのはあなたの行末。忘れられた私のことはかまわないが、お忘れになったあなたが、誓いの引き合いにされた神様の罰を受けて、いのちを落としてしまわれるのではないかと心配です。

三八
右近(うこん)

わすらるる身をば思はずちかひてし人のいのちの惜しくもあるかな

like the thin bamboo
hidden in fields of cogon-grass,
I have tried to hide my love,
but I can no longer restrain myself—
why do I long so much for you?

asajiu no ono no shinohara shinoburedo
amarite nado ka hito no koishiki   Sangi Hitoshi

Consultant Hitoshi

丈の低い茅のまばらに生えた広くもない野は、同時に篠竹の原でもあって、茅のあいだに隠れ忍ぶように篠竹が生えている。あたかもその篠竹のように隠れ忍ばせて来た私の思いもついに丈が余って忍びきれなくなってしまったらしい。どうしてこうもあの人が恋しくてならないのだろう。

三九
参議等(さんぎひとし)

浅茅生(あさぢふ)の小野(をの)のしのはらしのぶれどあまりてなどか人のこひしき

although I have tried
to hide my love in my heart,
it must show on my face—
people keep asking me
if I suffer from lovesickness

shinoburedo iro ni idenikeri waga koi wa
mono ya omou to hito no tou made　　Taira no Kanemori

Taira no Kanemori

誰にも気取られないようにひた隠しに隠して来た私の恋の思いだが、抑えすぎたあまり顔色に出てしまったのだろうか。もの思いでもなさっているのですか、と外でもない、思う相手に問われるまでに。ええ、あなたゆえのもの思いにねとも答えられず、私はどぎまぎするばかりだ。

四〇

平兼盛(たひらのかねもり)

しのぶれど色にいでにけりわが恋は物や思ふと人の問ふまで

already the rumour
is being whispered around
that I've fallen in love,
yet I have just begun
to yearn for you in secret

koisuchō wagana wa madaki tachinikeri
hitoshirezu koso omoisomeshi ka　　*Mibu no Tadami*

Mibu no Tadami

私が恋をしているという噂は、その恋がまだかたちを取ることのない、いわば恋の未明の闇のうちに立ってしまった。世の中の人は誰も、そう、思う相手の人も気づかぬほど、ひっそりと思いそめたばかりの、私のひめやかな恋だったのに。私に残されているのは、あらかじめ失われた恋の長く辛い一日だ。

四一
壬生忠見（みぶのただみ）

恋すてふわが名はまだき立ちにけり人知れずこそ思ひそめしか

do you not remember that we vowed,
as we wrung tears from our sleeves,
that the ocean waves
would never wash Sue's Pine Hill,
that our hearts would never change

chigirikina katami ni sode wo shiboritsutsu
sue no matsuyama nami kosaji to wa　　Kiyohara no Motosuke

Kiyohara no Motosuke

二人して固く約束したよねえ、お互いにお互いをいとしく思う涙に濡れた袖をしぼりながら、あの行末まで待ちつづけるという名の末の松山を波が越えるようなことは、けっしてけっしてありはしないと。まさかそのことを忘れたわけではあるまいに、あなたは。

四二
清原元輔（きよはらのもとすけ）

ちぎりきなかたみに袖をしぼりつつ末（すゑ）のまつ山浪こさじとは

compared to my heart
after spending a night with you,
my heart in the past,
before we met, hardly knew
the meaning of desperation

aimite no nochi no kokoro ni kurabureba
mukashi wa mono wo omowazarikeri   Gonchūnagon Atsutada

Acting Middle Counsellor Atsutada

恋いこがれて、しかし向かいあって逢うことの叶わなかったあなた。やっとのことに二人水入らずで逢って契りを結んだというのに、別れを惜しんで帰って来たばかりのこの切ない心持はいったいどうしたというのだろう。この気持ちに較べたら、一途に恋い焦がれた昔など、もの思いでも何でもなかったなあ。

四三
権中納言敦忠

あひ見ての後のこころにくらぶれば昔は物をおもはざりけり

had I never met her
I would not feel
this bitter resentment at all
for her abject indifference
nor for my desperation

aukoto no taeteshinakuwa nakanaka ni
hito wo mo mi wo mo uramizaramashi　　*Chūnagon Asatada*

Middle Counsellor Asatada

世の中に男と女の相逢うて契りを交わすということがまったくないものなら、その後でつめたくなったあなたを恨むことも、そんなあなたを慕わしく思って契りを結んでしまった自分を恨むこともあるまいに。しかし、それでも、そんなあなたがいよいよ慕わしく、そんな自分がいとおしく思われてならないとは。ああ、恋というものは。

四四

中納言朝忠(ちゅうなごんあさただ)

逢ふことの絶えてしなくはなかなかに人をも身をも恨みざらまし

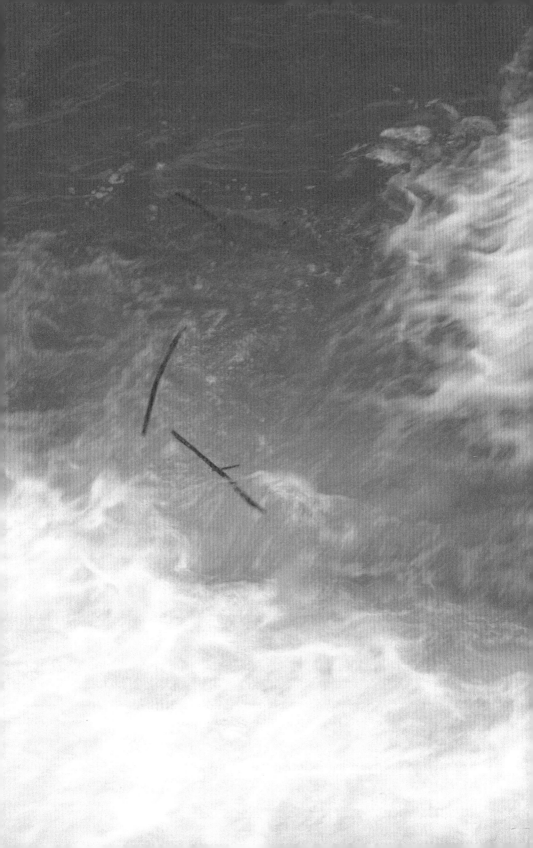

I cannot even think
of anyone who might
take pity and love me . . .
am I to die in vain
with this longing?

awaretomo iubeki hito wa omohoede
mi no itazura ni narinu beki kana　　*Kentokukō*

Lord Kentoku

恋いこがれた挙句、その思いの苦しさにこがれ死んでしまいそうな私。しかし、たといそんな結果になったとしても、かわいそうなことをしたと悲しんでくれる人があろうとは思われないので、私はきっとむだ死にに死んでしまうことになるのだろう。そうではありませんか、ねえあなた。

四五
謙徳公(けんとくこう)

あはれともいふべき人はおもほえで身のいたづらになりぬべきかな

a boatman
crossing Yura Strait,
has lost his rudder . . .
so, too, the passage of my love
knows no destination

yuranoto wo wataru funabito kaji wo tae
yukue mo shiranu koi no michi kana　　Sone no Yoshitada

Sone no Yoshitada

私はさながらあの波荒い由良の瀬戸を漕ぎわたろうとする舟人、荒波に取られて楫（かじ）を失い、行く方（ゆえ）もわからずにただゆらゆらとただよっていくほかはない。それが恋の大海原のたよりない道であり、その上をただようさだめない恋の小舟なのだ。

四六　曾根好忠(そねのよしただ)

由良(ゆら)の門(と)を渡る舟人かぢを絶えゆくへもしらぬ恋のみちかな

with its tangled growth of weeds
the estate looks desolate—
no visitor is coming
yet autumn
is my guest

yaemugura shigereru yado no sabishiki ni
hito koso miene aki wa kinikeri　　*Egyō Hōshi*

Priest Egyō

烈しい光の中、幾重にも葎が茂ったこの荒廃した邸は限りなくさびしいのに、誰ひとりとして訪ねてくる人もなく、代わりに秋が来てしまった、さびしさをさらに甚だしくする秋が。いや、そう嘆いている私も、それに頷いてくれている君たちもいる。そうでもなければ、さびしさに死んでしまうところだ。

四七
恵慶法師(えぎゃうほふし)

八重(やへ)むぐらしげれる宿のさびしきに人こそ見えね秋は来にけり

strong winds
shatter the waves
against unmoved rocks—
so, too, I suffer alone
from unreturned love

kaze wo itami iwa utsu nami no onore nomi
kudakete mono wo omou koro kana　　Minamoto no Shigeyuki

Minamoto no Shigeyuki

風が激しすぎて岩にぶつかる波がひとりでに砕け散る。ちょうどそのように恋しい人を思ってわれから砕け散らんばかりの今日このごろ。しかし、岩さながらのかの人は、私を砕け散らせておいて、自分はまるで知らんぷりなのだ。

四八
源(みなもとの)重之(しげゆき)

風をいたみ岩うつ浪のおのれのみくだけてものを思ふころかな

at the Imperial Palace gate,
the watch fires built in iron baskets
burn through the night like my desire,
then go out in daylight
like my discouraged heart

mikakimori eji no taku hi no yoru wa moe
hiru wa kietsutsu mono wo koso omoe　Ōnakatomi no Yoshinobu no Ason

Ōnakatomi no Yoshinobu, Court Noble

帝の在す宮居を幾重にも囲む御垣を守るべく、広く諸国の津津浦浦から集められた屈強の衛士たち、彼らが焚くかがり火は暗い夜を激しく燃えつづけ、昼は消えている。あたかもその火のように、私は恋の思いのために夜は苦しみ悶え、昼ともなれば意気消沈して死んでしまうばかりだ。

四九

大中臣能宣朝臣(おほなかとみのよしのぶのあそん)

みかきもり衛士(ゑじ)のたく火の夜はもえ昼は消えつつものをこそ思へ

I thought before
that I would give my life
for one night with you,
but now that we have met
I wish to live on and on

kimi ga tame oshikarazarishi inochi sae
nagaku mogana to omoinuru kana　　*Fujiwara no Yoshitaka*

Fujiwara no Yoshitaka

あなたを一途に思い、あなたへの思いが成就（じょうじゅ）するためになら私のいのちなど惜しくもないと思って来た私です。しかし、あなたへの思いをとげたいまとなっては、こんどはあなたに逢うためにいのちを大切にし、できるだけ長く生きたいと思う。恋とは、いのちとは、じつに不思議なものですね。

五〇
藤原義孝
ふぢはらのよしたか

君がため惜しからざりしいのちさへ長くもがなと思ひぬるかな

how I wish to confess
my burning desire, but I cannot—
just as moxa herbs from Ibuki smolder
you may never suspect
my ardent passion

kaku to dani eyawaibuki no sashimogusa
sashimo shirajina moyuru omoi wo   Fujiwara no Sanekata no Ason

Fujiwara no Sanekata, Court Noble

こんなにもあなたのことを思い悶悶の日夜を送っていますとだけでも伝えたいのですが、言葉にして伝えることなどどうしてできましょうか。伊吹山のさしも草の艾火のようにこもってわれとわが身を焦がす私の思いを、それほどまでとはとてもあなたはご存知ありますまい。

五一
藤原実方朝臣(ふぢはらのさねかたのあそん)

かくとだにえやはいぶきのさしも草さしもしらじな燃ゆる思(おもひ)を

when the day breaks
I know that night will fall again,
yet how disappointing
this morning glow is
after spending this night with you

akenureba kururu mono to wa shirinagara
nao urameshiki asaborake kana   *Fujiwara no Michinobu no Ason*

Fujiwara no Michinobu, Court Noble

朝が来て夜が明けたら、昼が過ぎてまた日が暮れ夜が来る、それが一日のならいと知ってはいますが、それでもなお、あなたと別れなければならない、またあなたと会うためには日が暮れるのを待たなければならない、そう思うとこの朝のほのぼの明けが恨めしくてならないのです。

五二

藤原道信朝臣(ふぢはらのみちのぶのあそん)

明けぬれば暮るるものとはしりながらなほ恨めしき朝ぼらけかな

grieving alone in bed,
the time until dawn
passes ever so slowly,
but you, alas,
will never know

nagekitsutsu hitori nuru yo no akuru ma wa
ikani hisashiki mono to kawa shiru　Udaishō Michitsuna no Haha

The Mother of the Commander of the Right Michitsuna

あなたにほかに思う女がいると聞いて、いかにも門は閉じていました。けれども、その独り寝の床でまんじりともせずに起きていて、あなたが門を言いわけのように叩いてあの女の許に行ってしまわれた後も、夜が明けるまでそのままでした。独り寝の女の夜の明けるまでがどんなに長いものか、殿方はおわかりでしょうか。おわかりにはなりますまい。

五三
右大将道綱母(うだいしゃうみちつなのはは)

なげきつつひとりぬる夜の明くるまはいかに久しき物とかはしる

your vow
to never forget me
cannot be trusted for my lifetime—
thus I crave to make today
the last day of my life

wasureji no yukusue made wa katakereba
kyō wo kagiri no inochi to mo gana   Gidōsanshi no Haha

The Mother of Associate Minister

あなたは私のことをけっして忘れることはないとおっしゃってくださる。そのお気持を信じないというわけではありませんが、お気持の行末いつまでも続くことがむつかしいのが世の慣い。それなら、そうおっしゃっていただいた倖せを永遠にするために、今日限りでいのちが終わってくれればいい、と思う私なのです。

五四
儀(ぎ)同(どう)三(さん)司(し)母(のはは)

忘れじの行末(ゆくすゑ)まではかたければ今日を限りの命ともがな

the waterfall's sound
has ceased now
for many ages,
yet its fame flows on
and still is heard today

taki no oto wa taete hisashiku narinuredo
na koso nagarete nao kikoekere　*Dainagon Kintō*

Grand Counsellor Kintō

かの歴史に聳え立つ輝かしい帝王、嵯峨上皇が営まれた嵯峨離宮はこの大覚寺となり、かつて豊かな水量を落としとどろかせた滝も絶えてより長い年月が経ってしまった。しかし、その名声は幻の滝音となっていまなお聞こえてくる。ならば、その幻の名滝をたたえるこの歌も、願わくは名声を得て、幾久しく伝わってほしいものだ。

五五
大納言公任(だいなごんきんたふ)

滝の音は絶えて久しくなりぬれど名こそ流れてなほきこえけれ

after my passing
into the other world,
for a memory to cherish,
I wish to see you
just once more

arazaran konoyo no hoka no omoide ni
ima hitotabi no au koto mogana　　Izumi Shikibu

Izumi Shikibu

この病み衰えたわが身を思いますのに、私は間もなく死んでいなくなってしまいましょう。明日はこの世の外なるあの世にいるわが身ですが、せめてそこで思い出すことができますように、いまひとたびあなたにお逢いしたい。きっと、きっといらっしゃっていただけますわね。

五六
和泉式部(いづみしきぶ)

あらざらむこの世のほかの思ひ出にいまひとたびのあふこともがな

we met again by chance
but before I could tell
if it was really you,
the midnight moon vanished
into the clouds

meguriaite mishi ya sore tomo wananu ma ni
kumogakurenishi yowa no tsukikage　Murasaki Shikibu

Murasaki Shikibu

一別以来永らく会うことのなかった幼馴染みのあなた、やっとめぐり逢えたうれしさも束の間、夜半には沈んでしまう月のようにあたふたと帰ってしまいましたね。残された私としてはほんとうに逢えたのかしらと、疑いたくなるあわただしさ。いまは月の光もない暗がりにぼんやりいる私です。

五七
紫式部

めぐり逢ひて見しやそれともわかぬまに雲がくれにし夜半の月かげ

near Mount Arima,
Ina's field of bamboo grass
sways with the wind,
and now so do I—
how can I forget you?

arimayama ina no sasahara kaze fukeba
ide soyo hito wo wasure yawa suru　　*Daini no Sanmi*

Daini no Sanmi

有馬山と猪名野とは万葉のむかしから聞こえた歌枕。有るといわれても否と答えたくなるようなささやかな篠原でも、風が吹いてくればそよぐもの。さあ、そのとおり、あてにならない殿方でも、どうして忘れたりなんぞしましょうか。声をかけられれば騒ぐ、それが女ごころというものですよ。

五八
大弐三位(だいにのさんみ)

ありま山ゐなの篠原(ささはら)かぜ吹けばいでそよ人を忘れやはする

if I had known you would not come,
I would have gone to bed earlier,
but now, I have stayed up late
watching the moon
till it fell in the west

yasurawade nenamashi mono wo sayo fukete
katabuku made no tsuki wo mishi kana　　*Akazome Emon*

Akazome Emon

きっと行くからとおっしゃって、けっきょくあなたはいらっしゃってはくださいませんでした。最初からそうとわかっていたら、ためらうことなく寝てしまったでしょうに、あなたをむなしく待ちつづけ、とうとう西の山の端に沈むまで憂い顔の月を見つづけてしまったことです。

五九 赤染衛門(あかぞめゑもん)

やすらはで寝なましものを小夜(さよ)ふけて傾(かた)ぶくまでの月を見しかな

the road to Mount Ōe, Ikuno fields,
and to Heaven's Ladder is so very long—
I haven't yet travelled the path,
nor have I seen
a letter from mother

Ōeyama ikuno no michi no tōkereba
mada fumi mo mizu ama no hashidate　　*Koshikibu no Naishi*

Koshikibu no Naishi

このたびの歌合に歌を召されたことで、歌の上手のお母さんからの代作は届きましたか、などとあなたはいたずらっぽくおっしゃる。けれど母のいる丹後の国府は山城と丹波の国境の大江山やら生野やら山野を越えて遠いところ、そこの名勝として聞こえた天橋立を踏んでみたこともありませんし、もちろん母からの手紙も見ていません。それにしても天橋立、じっさいにこの足で踏んでみたいなあ。母にも逢いたいなあ。

六〇
小式部内侍(こしきぶのないし)

大江山いくのの道の遠ければまだふみも見ずあまの橋立(はしだて)

eightfold cherry blossoms
from the ancient capital of Nara—
today they bloom beautifully,
glowing in the sun
in this ninefold Imperial Palace

inishie no nara no miyako no yaezakura
kyō kokonoe ni nioinuru kana　　Ise no Taifu

Ise no Taifu

かつて咲く花の匂うがごとく繁栄を誇った奈良の古都から、その地で育まれた桜の中でもことにめずらしい八重桜が、ここ平安京の宮中に届けられ、九重の皇居にふさわしくひときわ美しく咲き匂っている。なんとめでたく、うれしいことではございませんか。

六一 伊勢大輔(いせのたいふ)

いにしへの奈良の都の八重(やへ)ざくらけふ九重(ここのへ)ににほひぬるかな

while it is yet dark,
your crowing like a rooster
may deceive some folks,
but not Meeting Hill's gate guards
who still will bar your passage

yo wo komete tori no sorane wa hakaru tomo
yo ni ōsaka no seki wa yurusaji   Sei Shōnagon

Sei Shōnagon

さんざん長話で気を持たせたあげく、まだ夜も明けない深夜のうちにあたふた帰って夜の声にせかされてなどと下手な言いわけをなさり、おや函谷関のおつもり？とお尋ねすると、逢坂の関ですよとうまく切り返したとお思いかもしれませんが、男女の仲につながる逢坂の関ならなおのこと、やすやす通りぬけは叶いますまいよ。

六二

清少納言(せいせうなごん)

夜をこめて鳥のそらねははかるともよに逢坂の関はゆるさじ

all I wish for now is a way
to say, in my own words, face to face,
and not through a messenger,
that I resign myself
to giving up our love

ima wa tada omoitaenan to bakari wo
hitozute narade iu yoshi mogana   Sakyō no Daibu Michimasa

The Left City Commissioner Michimasa

私があなたの許に通っていることが人の知るところとなり、私はあなたのことをいまや思い切るよりほかしかたがなくなった。しかし、せめてその思い切るということを、人づてでなくこの身みずからあなたに真向かって伝えたいものだ。たといそれっきりで、以後はまったく会えないにしても。

六三
左京大夫道雅（さきゃうのだいぶ みちまさ）

今はただ思ひ絶えなむとばかりを人づてならでいふよしもがな

the fog begins to clear
at dawn over the river Uji,
revealing the stakes
for wickerwork fishing nets
in the shallows here and there

asaborake uji no kawagiri taedae ni
arawarewataru seze no ajirogi   Gonchūnagon Sadayori

Acting Middle Counsellor Sadayori

冬の朝のしらじら明け、旅の宿りから外に出てみると、立ちこめた川霧があちこち切れて、その霧の絶え間絶え間からあの瀬この瀬の網代木がしだいにくっきりと見えてくる。人麻呂の歌から「宇治十帖」の物語まで、なんとゆかしい宇治川の眺めではないか。

六四
権中納言定頼

朝ぼらけ宇治の川霧たえだえにあらはれわたる瀬瀬のあじろ木

bitterness and sorrow
keep my sleeves wet with tears,
yet they haven't been ruined—
more to be pitied
is my love-wrecked reputation

uramiwabi hosanu sode dani aru mono wo
koi ni kuchinan na koso oshikere　Sagami

Sagami

人のつれなさを恨み悲しみ、わが身のつらさを侘び嘆いて、涙をぬぐうこともたびたび。濡れどおしで干す気にもなれないこの袖もいつか朽ちてしまおうことさえ悔しいのに、その上この恋の結果立つ噂に私の名まで朽ち果てようとは、こんな口惜しいことがありましょうか。

六五
相模(さがみ)

恨みわびほさぬ袖だにあるものを恋に朽ちなむ名こそをしけれ

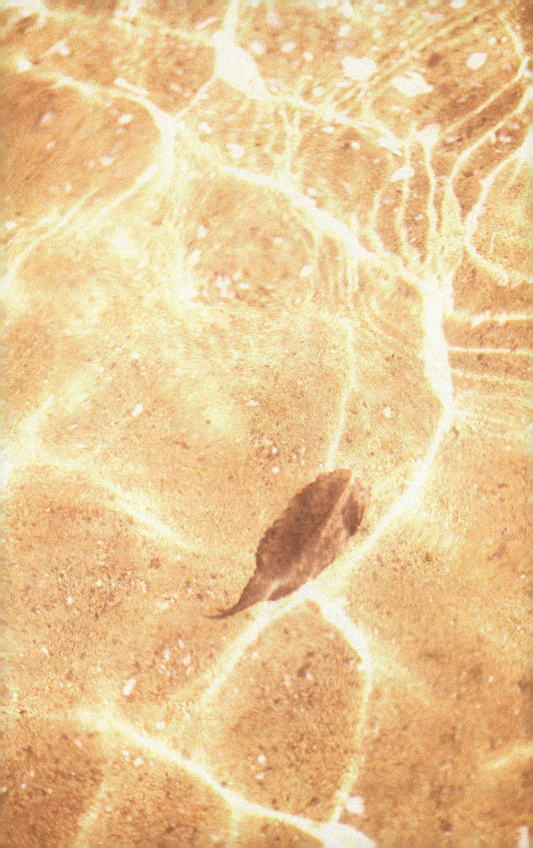

join me, please,
mountain cherry tree,
in thinking akin of each other—
I have no one but your blossoms
to share my heart

morotomo ni aware to omoe yamazakura
hana yori hoka ni shiruhito mo nashi　　Saki no Daisōjō Gyoson

Former Archbishop Gyōson

おたがいにしみじみなつかしいものに思いあおうではないか、山桜よ、この人里離れた山奥で修行する身にとっては、花であるお前のほかに私の心を知る人など、ありはしないのだから。

六六
前(さきの)大(だい)僧(そう)正(じゃう)行(ぎゃう)尊(そん)

もろともにあはれと思へ山ざくら花よりほかに知る人もなし

for this brief spring night's dream
your faithless arm
could pillow my head—
yes, but how pointless the loss
of my reputation

harunoyo no yume bakari naru tamakura ni
kainaku tatan na koso oshikere   Suō no Naishi

Suō no Naishi

そうでなくともはかない夢のような春の夜です。せっかくさし出してくださった勿体ないあなたの腕の手枕ですが、お借りしたばかりにつまらない浮名が立つようなことになって口惜しい限り。どうかお戯れはお引っこめくださいましな。

六七
周防内侍(すおうのないし)

春の夜のゆめばかりなる手枕(たまくら)にかひなく立たむ名こそ惜しけれ

although it is not my desire
to live longer
in this miserable world,
if I do, I will surely yearn
for tonight's moon

kokoro nimo arade ukiyo ni nagaraeba
koishikarubeki yowa no tsuki kana　　*Sanjōin*

Retired Emperor Sanjō

一天万乗という位にあっても、いやむしろその位にあるからこそ、諸事不如意のこの憂世。位を去りたいばかりかこの世にも別れたい思いだが、もしこの内心の願いにもかかわらず生き長らえることにでもなったら、今宵ここで不自由な目で眺めた真夜中の入りぎわの月が、さぞ恋しく思い出されるにちがいない。

六八
三条院
（さんでうゐん）

心にもあらでうき世にながらへば恋しかるべき夜半の月かな

a storm blowing
the tinted maple leaves
of Mount Mimuro
has made a rich brocade
on the river Tatsuta

arashi fuku mimuro no yama no momijiba wa
tatsuta no kawa no nishiki narikeri　　Nōin Hōshi

Monk Nōin

つい先立って三室の山のふもとを通りかかった折、はげしくあらしが吹き荒れて山の紅葉（もみじ）という紅葉が吹きちぎられ空に舞いくるっていたっけが、いま龍田の川のほとりを通りかかると川づらいっぱいに流れていく。なるほど、あの折のあらしは紅葉を折り込んで龍田の川の錦の長布（ながぬの）を織り出す秋の女神の手わざだったのだ、といまにしてわかった。

六九
能因法師(のういんほふし)

あらし吹く三室(みむろ)の山のもみぢばは龍田(たつた)の川のにしきなりけり

overcome by loneliness
I step out from my hut,
but when I look around,
everywhere it is the same
autumn dusk

sabishisa ni yado wo tachiidete nagamureba
izuko mo onaji aki no yūgure   Ryōzen Hōshi

Monk Ryōzen

庵(いおり)にこもっていて淋しさ極まり、居ても立ってもいられなくなり戸外に出て眼路(めじ)の限り見渡してみたが、どこも同じ秋の夕暮。この淋しさはわが心から出た淋しさと納得し、庵の中に帰って来た。そうと気づけば、しだいに濃さを増す秋の夕暮の中で、その淋しさもまたしみじみと親しく思えて来る。

七〇
良暹法師
りゃうぜんほふし

さびしさに宿を立ちいでてながむればいづこもおなじ秋のゆふぐれ

when evening comes
the ripe rice plants at my gate
make a rustling sound . . .
and the autumn wind blows
against my reed-thatched hut

yū sareba kadota no inaba otozurete
ashi no maroya ni akikaze zo fuku   Dainagon Tsunenobu

Grand Counsellor Tsunenobu

ここ、都を遠く離れて訪れる人とてもない山里ですが、それでも夕方ともなると、門前の田の繁った稲の葉をさやさや音たてて訪れたかと思うと、たちまち通りすぎ、この芦葺きの田舎家に吹きとどいている。これぞまさしく惚れっぽく飽きっぽい、その名のとおり秋風なのですね。

七一
大納言経信(だいなごんつねのぶ)

夕されば門田(かどた)の稲葉(いなば)おとづれてあしのまろやに秋風ぞ吹く

the waves washing
Takashi's famous shore
are high and capricious,
but I will not let them
splash and drench my sleeves

oto ni kiku takashi no hama no adanami wa
kakeji ya sode no nure mo koso sure   Yūshi Naishinnō-ke no Kii

Yūshi Naishinnō-ke no Kii

世に評判の高い高師の浜の、いたずらに高く寄せてはまた返るあだ波、まさにそう申すがぴったりの移り気なあなたの実のない誘い言葉を、心にかけるのはよしにしておきましょう。どうせ結果はこの袖が濡れるばかり。いえ、あなたの心の波のしぶきにではなく、捨てられた私みずからの涙に、ね。

七二　祐子内親王家紀伊

音に聞く高師の浜のあだ波はかけじや袖のぬれもこそすれ

on the ridge
of distant high mountains,
the cherry trees have bloomed—
I wish that the foothill haze
will not rise too high

takasago no onoe no sakura sakinikeri
toyama no kasumi tatazu mo aranan   Saki no Gonchūnagon Masafusa

Former Acting Middle Counsellor Masafusa

ここ都のうちから見わたすと、あの奥山の高い峰の上にも桜が咲きさかっている。むろん近景の端山は花が終わって霞が立つ頃だが、そのせいで、遠景の春の名残りが隠されて愉しめなくなるのは残念至極。外山の霞よ、なんとか大臣の家のめでたい宴の今日ばかりは立たないでいてほしいものだが。

七三
前権中納言匡房

高砂の尾上のさくら咲きにけり外山のかすみ立たずもあらなむ

I pine for her in vain,
oh mountain wind from Hatsuse,
yet I did not pray to the kannon
to make her more harsh,
but to blow her to me

ukarikeru hito wo hatsuse no yamaoroshi yo
hageshikare to wa inoranu mono wo   Minamoto no Toshiyori no Ason

Minamoto no Toshiyori, Court Noble

そもそもの初めからつれなく逢ってくれようともしないあの人を、思い果てようか、いや何とか逢ってやる気になってくれないものかと、恋の霊験あらたかな初瀬の観世音菩薩に参籠した。あれは冬だったが、その夜一夜吹き荒れていた山おろしの風よ、お前の激しさながら、あの人のつれなさがいっそう激しくなるようにと祈願したわけではないものを、以後の私はますます辛い恋の冬の嵐の最中にいる。

七四

源俊頼朝臣(みなもとのとしよりのあそん)

うかりける人を初瀬(はつせ)の山おろしよはげしかれとはいのらぬものを

your promise,
as fragile as dew on a mugwort leaf,
has kept me alive,
but this year's autumn, too,
seems to pass in vain

chigiriokishi sasemo ga tsuyu wo inochi nite
aware kotoshi no aki mo inumeri   Fujiwara no Mototoshi

Fujiwara no Mototoshi

けっして忘れはせぬ、とあれほど堅くお誓いくださいました蓬の葉の上の露のように甘やかなお言葉をいのちとも頼み、待ちこがれてまいりました私ですのに、はかなやお言葉は叶えられぬままに、ことしの秋も行ってしまおうとしております。やがて私のもとには冬が訪れて、蓬葉は枯れ、その上にはしらじらと霜が降りましょう。

七五

藤原基俊(ふぢはらのもととし)

契(ちぎ)りおきしさせもが露を命(いのち)にてあはれことしの秋もいぬめり

as I row out
onto the flat ocean,
the white wave-crests
blend in the distance
with the heavenly clouds

watanohara kogiidete mireba hisakata no
kumoi ni magau okitsushiranami   Hosshōji no Nyūdō Saki no Kanpaku Dajōdaijin

The Hosshōji Novice, Former Regent and Chancellor

この小さな舟の櫓櫂を取り、広びろとひらけた大海原に漕ぎ出してみると、はるか沖に立つ白波は水平線に立ちのぼる雲と見分けがつかない。よろず大切なのはこの距離。じゅうぶんな距離を持って眺望してみるならば、ここな貴い雲居にも何やらよくわからぬ怪しげな白波が立って畏き辺りを擾しているような。ゆめゆめご油断めさるな。

七六

法性寺入道前関白太政大臣

わたの原こぎいでてみればひさかたの雲居にまがふ沖つ白波

the swift current
blocked by a boulder
splits but meets again—
so too do I wish to be
one with you again

se wo hayami iwa ni sekaruru takigawa no
warete mo sue ni awan to zo omou   Sutokuin

Retired Emperor Sutoku

己という瀬の流れが直情すぎ性急すぎるからだろうか、世間という岩に堰かれ遮られて、激ち走る川のようなわが内心の事と志とは二つに、別れ別れを余儀なくされてしまった。しかしこれで退く私ではないぞ。かならずや行末、志を事と一つにして見せよう。たといそれが流離ののち、憤死ののちであるにしても。

七七
崇徳院(すとくゐん)

瀬を早み岩にせかるる滝川のわれても末にあはむとぞ思ふ

from Awaji Island,
the plovers visit and cry—
for how many nights
have I, Suma's barrier keeper,
been kept awake?

awajishima kayou chidori no naku koe ni
ikuyo nezamenu suma no sekimori　Minamoto no Kanemasa

Minamoto no Kanemasa

外の闇の中、波のむこうから通ってくる千鳥たち、暁ごとのその鳴き声に寝ざめて眠ることのできなかったという源氏の君は、申すなら精神上の須磨の関守。それから幾世をへだてた都住みの私も、末の世の須磨の関守として、闇の中の淡路島を幻視し、そこから通って来る千鳥の声を幻聴し、いくたびも寝ざめるのです。いとしい女よ。

七八
源兼昌

淡路島かよふ千鳥のなく声にいく夜ねざめぬ須磨の関守

breaking through
an opening in the clouds
that trail on the autumn wind—
how clear and pure
the moonlight

akikaze ni tanabiku kumo no taema yori
moreizuru tsuki no kage no sayakesa　Sakyō no Daibu Akisuke

The Left City Commissioner Akisuke

ふと秋風が吹きおこり、それまで大空いちめんにたなびいていた雲がいっしゅん切れた。と、その切れ間からもれ出た月の光の、なんというすがすがしい明るさ。雲一つなく晴れわたった空の中なら、かえってこれほどには身にしみることはあるまいと思われる今宵の月のさやけさなのだ。

七九
左京大夫顕輔（さきやうのだいぶあきすけ）

秋風にたなびく雲の絶間（たえま）よりもれいづる月のかげのさやけさ

I cannot know how long
your heart will stay unchanged—
my thoughts this morning
are as tangled as my black hair
after a night with you

nagakaran kokoro mo shirazu kurokami no
midarete kesa wa mono wo koso omoe　　*Taiken Mon'in no Horikawa*

Taiken Mon'in no Horikawa

末永くとあなたはおっしゃってください
ます。そのお心が嘘いつわりとはつゆ思い
ませんが、心とは変わりやすいもの、あな
たとの関わりがほんとうに末長くつづくの
か、とても自信は持てません。とくにお別
れしたばかりの今朝は、寝乱れたこのいた
ずらに長い黒髪さながら、私の心も乱れに
乱れて、もの思いに現ないありさまです。

八〇
待賢門院堀河(たいけんもんゐんのほりかは)

長からむ心もしらず黒髪のみだれてけさは物をこそ思へ

the long-awaited cuckoo's cry—
as I turn to see
where it sang,
all I find is
the pale morning moon

hototogisu nakitsuru kata wo nagamureba
tada ariake no tsuki zo nokoreru　Gotokudaiji no Sadaijin

The Gotokudaiji Minister of the Left

ほととぎすの鳴きそうな夜、いまかいまかと待つうちについに夜が明けてしまった。今夜もとうとう駄目だったかとあきらめようとすると、キョッと一声。あわてて声のしたと思われる方角を見ると、うっすらと有明月が残っているのみ。聞いたと思ったその声すら、そら耳ではなかったかと思われるはかなさだ。ああ、待つということは。

八一

後徳大寺左大臣

ほととぎす鳴きつる方をながむればただ有明の月ぞのこれる

suffering from her indifference
and lamenting my heartbreak,
yet my life continues—
it is only my tears
that cannot bear such bitterness

omoiwabi sate mo inochi wa aru mono wo
uki ni taenu wa namida narikeri　　*Dōin Hōshi*

Monk Dōin

ものの思いのはてわが身をはかなんでいても、自分ではどうにもならないはずの生命(いのち)は、それでもしぶとく持ちこたえているのに、自分でどうにかなりそうな涙の方は、つらさに耐えかねて絶えあふれてくる。人間の生理とはなんというままならない、不可思議なものであることか。

八二
道因法師(だういんほふし)

思ひわびさても命(いのち)はあるものを憂きにたへぬは涙なりけり

from this world
we can never escape—
even deep in the mountains
where I come to contemplate,
the stag cries plaintively

yononaka yo michi koso nakere omoiiru
yama no oku nimo shika zo naku naru Kōtaigōgū no Daibu Shunzei

Commissioner of the Grand Empress' Household Office Shunzei

この世の男女関係には人としての道さえないのだと思いつめ、深く決心して山深く入って来たこの身だが、その山の奥にも妻呼ぶ鹿が悲しげに鳴いているようだ。どこに入っても俗世のはだしから逃げることなどできやしない。それならままよ、俗世に戻ってむしろ俗情にまみれて生きることにしようか。

八三

皇太后宮大夫俊成(くわうたいごうぐうのだいぶしゆんぜい)

世の中よ道こそなけれ思ひ入る山の奥にも鹿ぞ鳴くなる

should I live on,
I will fondly remember
this time of my life—
even the hard times of the past
are dear to me now

nagaraeba mata konogoro ya shinobaren
ushi to mishi yo zo ima wa koishiki　　*Fujiwara no Kiyosuke no Ason*

Fujiwara no Kiyosuke, Court Noble

人間関係に苦しみ運命に悩み、ほんとうに憂わしい毎日を送る今日この頃です。しかし、この苦悩は年とともに深まり、のちには今日この頃の苦悩がなつかしく思えるのではないでしょうか。かつての苦悩の日日が今日この頃に較べたらなつかしく思えるのですから。ああ、なんという人生か。

八四

藤原清輔朝臣

ながらへばまたこの頃やしのばれむ憂しと見し世ぞいまは恋しき

night after long night
as I lie pensively,
daybreak does not come easily—
even the gap between my bedroom doors
stays heartlessly dark

yomosugara monoomou koro wa akeyaranu
neya no hima sae tsurenakarikeri　Shun'e Hōshi

Preist Shun'e

一晩じゅう訪れのないあなたを思って、思い悩む今日この頃は、訪れてくださらないあなたのみか、いつまでも夜明けとなってくれない寝室の戸の隙間までが無情に思われてつらいことです。この長い秋の夜をあなたはいったい、どこのどんな女と睦言を交わしていらっしゃるのでしょうか。

八五
俊恵法師(しゆんゑほふし)

よもすがら物思ふころは明けやらぬ閨(ねや)のひまさへつれなかりけり

did the moon tell me
to lament my fate?
no, it did not,
yet my streaming tears
want to blame the moon

nageke tote tsuki ya wa mono wo omowasuru
kakochigao naru waga namida kana   Saigyō Hōshi

Monk Saigyō

目の前に澄みわたる耿耿(こうこう)と円(まど)かな月。その前にいての私のこのもの思いは、月が私に嘆けと言ってものを思わせるのか。いやいやけっしてそんなわけではない。そのことは重重わかっているのに、いけないいけない、つい月のせいにして託(かこ)つけがましくもあふれて頬(ほお)をつたう未練千万な涙よ。

八六
西行法師(さいぎゃうほふし)

なげけとて月やは物を思はするかこち顔なるわが涙かな

veiling the pine needles,
still wet with dew
from passing showers,
the fog rises high
this autumn twilight

murasame no tsuyu mo mada hinu maki no ha ni
kiri tachinoboru aki no yūgure　*Jakuren Hōshi*

Monk Jakuren

雨がひとしきりさっと降っては、通りすぎて行った。そのむらさめの露しずくがまだ乾きもやらぬ針葉樹の細かい葉の固まりごとに霧が立ちのぼってくる。と思うと、いつしか暮れて行く。なんとも定めなく、あわたゞしい秋の暮れがた。そこにいる私も人生の暮れがたにいる自分をひしひしと感じるのです。

八七
寂蓮法師（じゃくれんほふし）

むらさめの露もまだひぬ真木（まき）の葉に霧たちのぼる秋のゆふぐれ

just one night together,
brief as the joints between reeds
reaped from Naniwa Bay—
must I, for this faint love,
now sacrifice my life?

naniwae no ashi no karine no hitoyo yue
mi wo tsukushite ya koi wataru beki　　Kōka Mon'in no Bettō

Intendant at Kōka Mon'in

淀川の河口近い難波の入江では、秋ごとに芦を根元から刈るこの江口の里。その風景の見えるここ江口の里。気まぐれに立ち寄って私と仮寝の一夜を過ごしたにすぎないあなたのことが忘れられず、舟路を示して波に浮き沈みするあの澪標さながら、この身が尽きるまであなたを恋いつづけることになるのでしょうか。

八八
皇嘉門院別当

難波江の芦のかり寝のひと夜ゆゑみをつくしてや恋ひわたるべき

if the jeweled thread of life
is to be cut, then let it be cut—
for if I live on,
I may become too weak
to hide my secret love

tama no o yo taenaba taene nagaraeba
shinoburu koto no yowari mo zo suru   Shokushi Naishinnō

Princess Shokushi

みずから見たことはないが、わが魂をわが躰に結びつけているという美しいいのちの緒紐よ、切れるならいっそ切れてしまってくれ。こんなに苦しい気持のまま、これ以上生き存えても、いつしか心弱りして、せっかく忍び匿して来た裡の思いが外に現れてしまいかねないから。

八九

式子内親王(しょくしないしんわう)

玉の緒よ絶えなば絶えねながらへば忍ぶることの弱りもぞする

although drenched,
the sleeves of Ojima Island divers
never change their colour—
I wish to show you my sleeves
that run red from bloody tears

misebaya na ojima no ama no sode dani mo
nure ni zo nureshi iro wa kawarazu   Inpu Mon'in no Taifu

Inpu Mon'in no Taifu

お見せしたいものですわ。あなたを思う血の涙で色も変わってしまった私のこの袖。あなたは辛い涙に乾く間もない自分の袖に較べられるのは、あのみちのくの雄島の磯に漁りする漁師の、海水に濡れどおしの袖だけだ、とおっしゃいますが、その海水びたしの袖だって血の涙に染まっているわけではありますまいものね、恋の漁師さん。

九〇
殷富門院大輔(いんぷもんゐんのたいふ)

見せばやな雄島(をじま)のあまの袖だにもぬれにぞぬれし色はかはらず

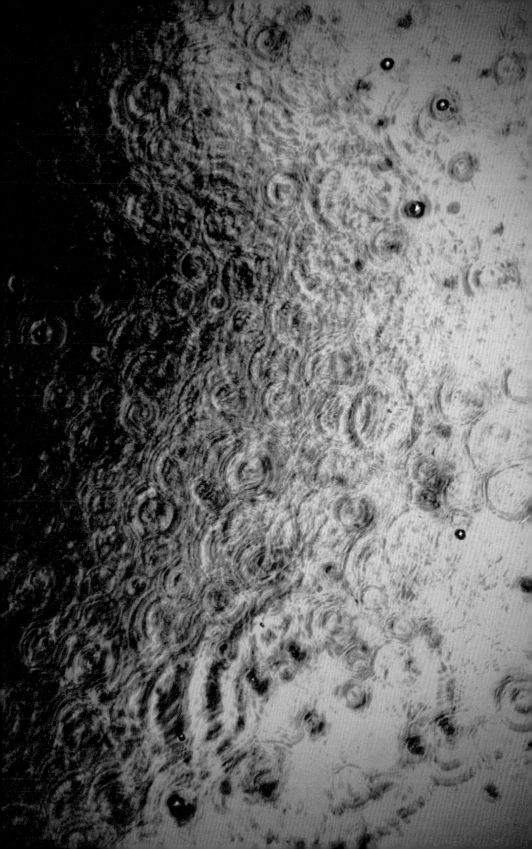

a cricket is chirping . . .
on the frosty night's cold rush mat,
am I to lie on a sleeve
of my own nightgown
and sleep alone?

kirigirisu naku ya shimoyo no samushiro ni
koromo katashiki hitori kamo nen　　*Gokyōgoku Sesshō Saki no Dajōdaijin*

The Go-Kyōgoku Regent and Former Chancellor

こおろぎがきれぎれに鳴く、この霜降る夜なか。私はあなたのいらっしゃるのを待ったあげく、このさむざむとした寝筵(ねむしろ)の上、思いあう同士たがいに袖敷きかわすこともなく、おのれひとりの衣を敷いてまたしても独り寝の夜をすごすのでしょうか。いいえ、心優しいあなたは、きっといつかは来てくださると信じていますよ。

九一

後京極摂政前太政大臣

きりぎりす鳴くや霜夜のさむしろに衣かたしきひとりかも寝む

my drooping sleeves
are like offshore rocks
hidden even at low tide,
thoroughly drenched with tears,
with never a chance to dry

waga sode wa shiohi ni mienu oki no ishi no
hito koso shirane kawaku ma mo nashi   Nijōin no Sanuki

Nijōin no Sanuki

私の着ている衣の袖は、たとえていえば潮が干た際にも波の下に沈んで見えないというあの沖の石。誰にも知られず、とりわけ思う当の相手のあなたにも気づかれることなく、片恋のつらい涙の海水の下に沈んで、乾くひますらないのです。

九二
二条院讃岐(にでうゐんのさぬき)

わが袖は潮干(しほひ)に見えぬ沖の石の人こそしらねかわくまもなし

I wish the world
to stay unchanged forever—
how stirring it is
to see a fisherman's rowboat
towed from along the shore

yononaka wa tsunenimo gamona nagisa kogu
ama no obune no tsunade kanashi mo   Kamakura no Udaijin

The Kamakura Minister of the Right

男女の仲にはじまって世はは無常といわれるが、常凡の人情としてはやはり常に変わらずあってほしいもの。常の穏やかな日なら渚をゆっくり漕いで行く漁師の小舟が、きょうは波が荒いからか、曳舟の曳綱に曳かれて行く。それをうち眺める自分とて、いつ運命の曳綱に曳かれないとも限らない無常の身だ。

九三
鎌倉右大臣

世のなかはつねにもがもな渚こぐあまの小舟の綱手かなしも

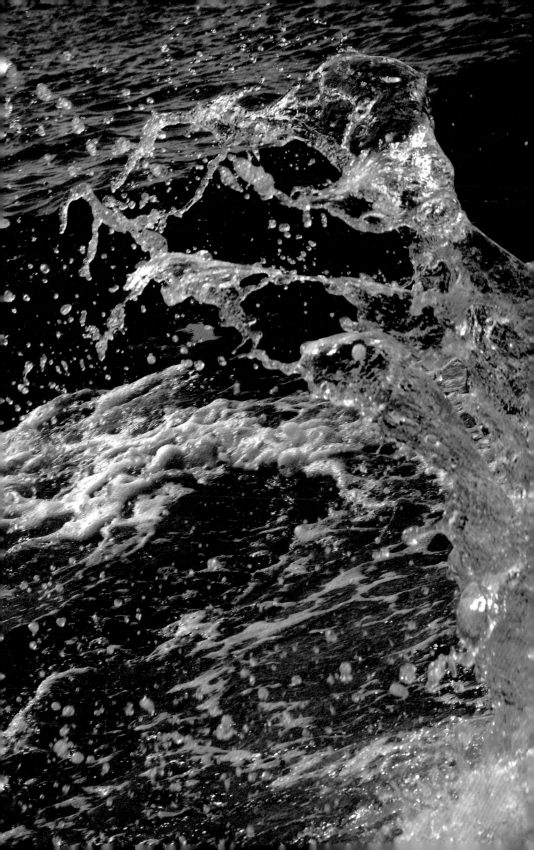

the autumn wind blows
from the mountains of Yoshino
deep into the night—
as the ancient capital grows colder
the villagers beat fabric into softness

miyoshino no yama no akikaze sayo fukete
furusato samuku koromo utsu nari　　Sangi Masatsune

Consultant Masatsune

　その昔、天皇の行幸が相次いだ吉野だが、いまはそのようなことも長く絶え、山から吹きおろす秋風の中、いつか夜も更けて衣打つ砧の音が寒寒と聞こえてくる。思い出されるのは唐の詩人、李太白の「万戸衣ヲ擣ツノ声」、おあつらえ向きに大都「長安」ならぬ、旧里吉野の「一片ノ月」も出ている。

九四
参議雅経(さんぎまさつね)

みよしのの山の秋かぜ小夜ふけてふるさと寒く衣うつなり

failing to know my place,
I wish to save people in this troubled world
as I start to dwell at Mount Hiei
by spreading out the black-dyed sleeves
of my monk's habit

ōkenaku ukiyo no tami ni ōu kana
waga tatsu soma ni sumizome no sode   *Saki no Daisōjō Jien*

Former Archbishop Jien

身のほど知らずにも、悩み多いこの世の万民の上におおいかけようと願うことだ、われらの祖師伝教大師（最澄）が「阿耨多羅三藐三菩提のほとけたちわがたつ杣に冥加あらせたまへ」（『新古今和歌集』巻二十釈教歌）と祈って開かれた比叡のみ山に住みそめたこの身につけている墨染の僧衣の袖を。み仏たちよ、どうかこの身にも冥加あらせたまえ。

九五
前大僧正慈円（さきのだいそうじゃうじゑん）

おほけなくうき世の民におほふかなわがたつ杣（そま）に墨染（すみぞめ）の袖

a windstorm tempts cherry blossoms
to scatter their petals over the garden—
no, it is not snow
that has fallen and accumulated
but my own age

hana sasou arashi no niwa no yuki narade
furiyuku mono wa wagami narikeri   Nyūdō Saki no Dajōdaijin

The Novice and Former Chancellor

咲きつくした花を誘うように春の嵐が吹き、花吹雪が舞い、庭いちめんに散り敷く。こうして花は古り、春も古り行くと、庭の最中に花の雪を浴びて立ちつくし、うたた感慨に耽っていた私だが、まことに古り行くものはわが身であったと気づかされた。さよう、春はまた巡り花はまた咲くが、人である私の花の盛りはふたたび訪れることがないのだ。

九六
入道前太政大臣

花さそふあらしの庭の雪ならでふりゆくものはわが身なりけり

I wait for my love in vain
in the suffocating evening calm
of Matsuho Bay
where seaweed is burnt for salt—
I too blaze with passion

konuhito wo matsuho no ura no yūnagi ni
yaku ya moshio no mi mo kogaretsutsu   *Gonchūnagon Teika*

Junior Second Rank Ietaka

待っても待っても、けっして来ることのないあなたを待ちつづけ、身も心も焼け焦がれる思いのわが身は、その名も松帆の浦の、昼日中は塩水をかけては乾され、夕べになれば、ひたとの風もない夕凪の中、海女たちに焼かれて焦がされる藻塩さながら。そうとわかっていても待たずにはいられない私なのです。

九七
権中納言定家

こぬ人をまつほの浦の夕なぎに焼くや藻塩の身もこがれつつ

oak leaves rustle in the breeze,
and the twilight at Nara Brook
is already chilly—
only ritual rinsings show
that summer is still here

kaze soyogu nara no ogawa no yūgure wa
misogi zo natsu no shirushi narikeru　*Junii Ietaka*

Junior Second Rank Ietaka

ここ平安京の地主神、賀茂別雷神を祀る上賀茂神社境内、楢の木の葉が風にそよぐならの小川の夕暮れどき。あたりの風情はすでに秋の気配だが、いましも夏越の祓がおこなわれているのを見ると、そこだけはまだかろうじて夏なのだ、と思い知られる。私たちはすでに秋にいるのか。それともまだ名残りの夏に？

九八
従二位家隆(じゅにゐいへたか)

風そよぐならの小川のゆふぐれはみそぎぞ夏のしるしなりける

people are dear
and also hateful—
in this disappointing world,
I am positioned to care
and to think of the way life is

hito mo oshi hito mo urameshi ajikinaku
yo wo omou yue ni monoomou mi wa   Gotobain

Retired Emperor Go-Toba

人よ、そなたのことがある時はいとしく、ある時はうらめしい。というのも、ただびとならば恋ゆえのもの思いに耽（ふけ）っていればすむものを、なまじ帝王の位にのぼったばかりに世間を相手の、およそ味気ないもの思いをしなければならないからだ。

九九　後鳥羽院(ごとばゐん)

人もをし人もうらめしあぢきなく世を思ふゆゑに物思ふ身は

under the old eaves
of the Imperial Palace,
memory ferns are thriving—
the glories of the old days
are ever more appealing

momoshiki ya furuki nokiba no shinobu nimo
nao amariaru mukashi narikeri   Juntokuin

Retired Emperor Juntoku

沢山の石を敷き詰めて築いた王朝の礎を盤石にしようと、百千に心を砕き企てを重ねてきたつもりだが、すべては水泡に帰してしまった。いまこの荒れ古びた、その上雨さえ降っている軒端の衰微のしるしのような忍草を見ていると、自分に残された営為は王朝の盛んだった昔を偲ぶことのみ。だからといって、輝かしい昔が帰って来るわけではないのだ。

一〇〇
順徳院

ももしきや古き軒端のしのぶにも猶あまりある昔なりけり

高岡一弥（たかおかかずや）　1945年、京都府生まれ。アートディレクター。主な著書に『千年』（毎日新聞社）、『野菜から見た肉』（パルコ出版）、『春・観る』（時事通信社）、『女性とエイズ』『Quality of Life』（日本財団）、『katachi』（ピエ・ブックス）、雑誌『活人』少女光線、日本未少年（毎日新聞社）。『彼方へ』『東京 LIVING WITH AIDS & HIV』等、展覧会イベントを主催。日宣美展特選、日本グラフィックデザイン展金賞、講談社出版文化賞受賞、他。

高橋睦郎（たかはしむつお）　1937年、北九州八幡に生まれ、翌年父を失う。母が各地に働きに出たため、親戚や他人の家を転々とし、孤独な中で言葉に親しむ。少年時代から詩、俳句、短歌、その他あらゆる詩形を試作し、現在に至る。24冊の詩集のほか、句集、歌集、小説集、評論集…など著書多数。また、演劇やオペラの台本、新作能、新作狂言など、舞台に関わり国内外での自作詩朗読にも力をそそぐ。詩集『兎の庭』で高見順賞、句歌集『稽古飲食』で読売文学賞、台本修辞『王女メディア』でグローバル国際交流基金山本健吉賞…など受賞多数。2000年度紫綬褒章受賞。文芸、芸能の発生および歴史に関心深く、『読みなおし日本文学史——歌の漂泊』『十二夜——闇と罪の王朝文学史』『遊ぶ日本——神あそぶゆえ人あそぶ』。俳句関係では『私自身のための俳句入門』『百人一句』などの著書がある。

伊藤之一（いとうゆきかず）　1966年、愛知県生まれ。カメラマン。主な写真集に、「入り口」「ヘソ」「テツオ」「電車カメラ」「ハレ」（共にWALL出版）がある。主な写真展に「溶ける箱」（ニエプスギャラリー）「SINSHOKU」（コダックフォトサロン）「入り口」（銀座ニコンサロン）「ハレ」（WALL）がある。

宮下惠美子（みやしたえみこ）　1954年、福島県福島市生まれ。イリノイ州とガーナ共和国のアクラで成長期の2年ずつを過ごす。同志社大学英文学科卒。有馬朗人主宰『天為』俳句会同人。俳人協会幹事。国際俳句交流協会評議委員。アメリカハイク協会、カナダハイク協会会員。『朝日ウイークリー』HAIKU欄選者。著書に『The New Pond: An English-language Haiku Anthology 新しい池：英語圏の俳人たち』、句集『たちまち』。翻訳に『山頭火』『Love Haiku: Masajo Suzuki's Lifetime of Love』、『Einstein's Century』、『俳句』、『和の菓子』、『能』、他。2002年度アメリカハイク協会メリットブック賞翻訳部門受賞。

Michael Dylan Welch（マイケル・ディラン・ウェルチ）　1962年、英国ワットフォード生まれ。米国ロマリンダ大学の英語学の文学修士課程終了。米国ワシントン州在住。俳句暦は30年、短歌暦もすでに20年を越える。1991年に始まる隔年開催の北米俳句大会Haiku North Americaの創設者の一人、1996年にはアメリカハイク文庫の創設に関わる。2000年にアメリカ短歌協会を創立し2004年まで会長を務める。前アメリカハイク協会副会長。Haiku Northwestグループ主宰。アメリカハイク協会会員、カナダハイク協会会員、ユウキテイケイ俳句協会会員、北カリフォルニア俳人協会会員、短詩誌「Tundra」編集発行人、短歌と俳句の出版社Press Here社主、『Haiku Anthology』（Norton, 1999）など多くの秀句選集に取り上げられ受賞句も多く、何ヶ国語にも翻訳された作品は広く親しまれている。

百人一首

2008年12月16日　初版第1刷発行

アートディレクション　高岡一弥
文・解説　髙橋睦郎
写真　伊藤之一

英訳　宮下惠美子
　　　マイケル・ディラン・ウェルチ

編集　高岡一弥
デザイン　伊藤修一　松田香月　黒田真雪
制作進行　瀧亮子

発行者　三芳伸吾
発行所　ピエ・ブックス
〒170-0005　東京都豊島区南大塚2-32-4
編集　TEL: 03-5395-4820　FAX: 03-5395-4821
　　　E-mail: editor@piebooks.com
営業　TEL: 03-5395-4811　FAX: 03-5395-4812
　　　E-mail: sales@piebooks.com
http://www.piebooks.com

印刷・製本　株式会社サンニチ印刷
Book and cover design © 2008 Kazuya Takaoka
Selection and Text copyright © 2008 Mutsuo Takahashi
Photographs copyright © 2008 Yukikazu Ito
English Text copyright © 2008 Emiko Miyashita and Michael Dylan Welch
Published by PIE BOOKS

本書の収録内容の無断転写、複写、引用等を禁じます。
落丁・乱丁はお取り替えいたします。

ISBN978-4-89444-757-8　C0072　Printed in Japan

郵 便 は が き

170 - 8790

038

料金受取人払郵便

豊島支店承認

7405

差出有効期間
平成22年3月
31日まで

東京都豊島区南大塚2-32-4
ピエ・ブックス 行

|||||||||||||||||||

アフターサービス・新刊案内・マーケティング資料・今後の企画の参考とさせていただきますので、お手数ですが各欄にご記入の上、お送りください。なお、ご記入いただいたデータは上記以外には使用いたしません。

1108 百人一首

(フリガナ) お名前		年齢	性別 **男・女**

ご住所　〒　　　　　　　　　　　TEL　　　（　　　）
e-mail

ご職業	購入店名

● いままでに読者カードをお出しいただいたことが　　1.ある　2.ない

ご購入書籍名をご記入ください。

```
┌─────────────────────────────────────┐
│                                     │
│                                     │
└─────────────────────────────────────┘
```

1. この本を何でお知りになりましたか
   1. 新聞・雑誌（紙・誌名　　　　　　　　　）　2. チラシ・ポスター
   3. 友人、知人の話　　4. 店頭で見て　　5. プレゼントされた
   6. 小社の新刊案内　　7. その他（　　　　　　　　　　　　）

2. この本についてのご意見、ご感想をお聞かせください。

   ………………………………………………………………………………
   ………………………………………………………………………………
   ………………………………………………………………………………
   ………………………………………………………………………………

3. よく購読されている雑誌名をお書き下さい。

● ………………………………………………………………………………
● ………………………………………………………………………………
● ………………………………………………………………………………

4. 今後、小社より出版をご希望の企画、テーマがありましたら、
   ぜひお聞かせください。

   ………………………………………………………………………………
   ………………………………………………………………………………
   ………………………………………………………………………………
   ………………………………………………………………………………

● アンケートにご協力いただきありがとうございました。　　1108 百人一首